NONVIOLENCE IN HAWAII'S SPIRITUAL TRADITIONS

Edited by

Glenn D. Paige and Sarah Gilliatt

Center for Global Nonviolence Planning Project
Spark M. Matsunaga Institute for Peace
University of Hawaii
Honolulu, Hawaii
96822

Manufactured in the United States America

Library of Congress Cataloging-in-Publication Data

Nonviolence in Hawaii's spiritual traditions / edited by Glenn D.
   Paige and Sarah Gilliatt
        p.   cm.
"These essays were first presented as brief talks given . . . on the
campus of the University of Hawaii at Manoa on January 11,
 1990." --pref.

   Includes bibliographical references and index.
   ISBN 1-880309-00-9 (alk. paper) : $5.00
   1. Nonviolence--Religious aspects. 2. Violence--Religious aspects. 3.
Hawaii--Religion. I. Paige, Glenn D. II. Gilliatt, Sarah.
BL65.V55N66 1991
291.5'697--dc20   91-36117
                                                       CIP

Religions are different roads
converging on the same point.

M.K. Gandhi

CONTENTS

Photo by Peter Miller

From left to right: Ira J. Lichton, Francine Blume, Wasim Siddiqui, Ruth Anna
Brown, Anna McAnany, Nahuanani Patrinos, Stanley Amos, Lou Ann Ha'aheo
Guanson, Tony Pelle, Yoshiaki Fujitani, Robert Aitken, Gurudeva Sivaya
Subramuniyaswami, Glenn D. Paige.

Preface

These essays were first presented as brief talks given in Kuykendall Auditorium on the campus of the University of Hawaii at Manoa on January 11, 1990. They were offered as contributions of the Center for Global Nonviolence Planning Project to celebrate the Hawaii State Martin Luther King Jr. Holiday Week in cooperation with the King Holiday Commission chaired by Dr. Donnis Thompson.

We are privileged to be able to present these insights into nonviolence in Hawaii's spiritual traditions and are deeply grateful to the authors for sharing them. We recognize, as does each of them, that interpretations can vary within each tradition. Therefore none of them claims to speak for all adherents of their faith. Nevertheless each voice is an authentic one and merits most thoughtful reception.

Each contributor was invited to address, if appropriate, one or more of the five principal questions that guide the research interests of the Global Nonviolence Planning Project. That is, of each spiritual tradition we asked for insights into (1) the causes of violence, (2) the causes of nonviolence, (3) the causes of transition between violence and nonviolence, (4) the characteristics of a completely nonviolent society, and (5) implications for action.

We recognize also that not all of Hawaii's faiths--and, of course, not all relevant world faiths--are represented here. We hope that those who wish to share insights into nonviolence in other traditions, as well as in the present ones, will contribute them so that future presentations can assist greater breadth and depth of understanding. What we have demonstrated here locally can be done in other societies and indeed globally.

We hope that the people of Hawaii, visitors to Hawaii, and people everywhere will find this little book useful in reflecting upon the roots of respect for life in their own spiritual and humanist traditions. For it is out of such roots that the promise grows of realizing a nonviolent society in Hawaii and in the world. Against divisive violence, these essays affirm nonviolent spiritual community.

We hereby record respectful appreciation to all those who helped to make this exploration of nonviolent culture possible, including the Faculty Council of the Spark M. Matsunaga Institute for Peace, Francine Blume, Lou Ann Ha'aheo Guanson, Peter Miller, Christine Nahuanani Patrinos S.N.J.M., and the people of Hawaii. We are indebted to Stanley Schab for technical assistance. Publication has been made possible in part through the generosity of Professor Theodore L. Herman, Director Emeritus of Peace Studies, Colgate University, and founder of the Nonviolence Study Group, International Peace Research Association.

Glenn D. Paige
Sarah Gilliatt

Honolulu
August 1991

Hawaiian

Lou Ann Haʻaheo Guanson

'O nā Kumu akua a pau i hānau 'ia i ka Pō
  i ka Lā hiki kū;
   Ea mai ke kai mai!
    'O nā Kumu ali'i a pau i hānau 'ia i ka Pō
     i ka Lā hiki kū;
      Ea mai ke kai mai!
   'O nā Lālā ali'i a pau i hānau 'ia i ka Pō
  i ka Lā hiki kū;

Ea mai ke kai mai.
'O nā Wēlau ali'i a pau i hānau 'ia i ka Pō

  i ka Lā hiki kū;

  Ea mai ke kai mai!
  'O nā Pua ali'i a pau, E kū e ola
A kau a kaniko'o, pala lau hala

Haumaka'iole Kolopupū!

Oh original gods born in remote antiquity where the sun rises, Rise up out of the sea! Oh original chiefs, born in remote antiquity in the sunrise, Arise from the sea! Oh relatives of all the chiefs born in remote antiquity in the sunrise, Arise from the sea! Oh distant kin of all the chief born in remote antiquity where the sun rises, Arise from the sea! Oh descendents of the chief, Stand up and live! Live to remote old age! Stand until the support of a cane is needed![1]

1

The Hawaiian traditions were passed
on orally through the prayers and chants
of the people. To fully appreciate the depth of the
tradition, one must hear the melodic sounds of the voices.
Here, an attempt is made to convey in written form the oral
traditions of the Hawaiians.

The spiritual traditions of the Hawaiians are integrated into the
Hawaiian culture. Their spirituality and everyday life are
woven together, *Ua hilo 'ia i ke aho a ke aloha,*
"braided with the cords of love." The Hawaiians
are gentle natured people living in deep
spirituality with the land. Their
gentleness is reinforced by the
communal life on an island. Their
spirituality is strengthened by the
land and other elements of nature.
The prayers and chants of the
Hawaiians acknowledge the divine
spirits within all people and the
things around them.

In the Hawaiian religious tradition
there exists a universal equilibrium
between humanity and nature to
maintain the harmony in heaven and
on earth. To maintain this equilibrium,
the Hawaiians worship many gods. The
gods provide qualities and values to guide the
people. The gods Kāne, Kū, Lono, and Hina
exemplify important principles and values to the people.

Kāne, the leading god, is known as the creator of humanity,
symbol of life and nature, god of fresh water and sunlight and
forests. He is the giver of life. He possesses the qualities of
benevolence and creativity. Kāne represents the omnipresence
of the divine spirit of nature and the interconnectedness of nature
and humanity.

Kū, meaning upright, represents male generating powers. Kū is the god of war, both offensive and defensive. More important is the defensive role of protector and defender of the people. Kū exemplifies the values of respect, pride, moral courage, and valor. His responsibilities include rain, fishing, sorcery, and planting. Since his generative powers are more important than war, Kū is symbolized by the agricultural tool, the *ō'ō* (digging stick) which, at one time, was functional for economic development and productivity.

Lono, the god of peace, exemplifies healing, mercy and hospitality. During *makahiki*, a four month festival, Lono outlaws war. He represents and achieves the people's desire for peace. In addition, Lono is considered the god of clouds, winds, rain, and fertility. In this capacity, he symbolizes giving and generosity.

Hina, the god of female generative powers of fertility, was the counterpart of Kū as the expression of male generative powers. Hina expresses energies of reproduction and growth. Kū is erect; Hina is supine. Hina is the left hand; Kū is the right. Hina is one of the major gods of medicine and fishing. Hina and Kū represent the equilibrium and harmony for well being.

The principles and values of the gods are emulated by the people. In their worship they live these values daily and integrate the values into their way of life. The deep spirituality of the Hawaiians of the past help to maintain a consistent state of prayer. As the Hawaiians looked at the beauty of the flowers or the richness of the soil, they were in prayer with the gods. Mary Kawena Pukui states that the Hawaiians were *haipule*, religious. "Everything they did, they did with prayer." The lessons from the gods are taught and passed on in the oral tradition. The following is a pule (prayer) to the gods asking for wisdom and power:

E 'Io ē, e 'Io ē,   O 'Io, o 'Io,
E kū, e manu ē   O stand, o bird
Ke alu aku nei ka pule iā *Hakalau*   Combine prayers to
                                 overcome *haku-lau*
Kūlia ka lani iā *Uli*   The heavens-high-one
                                 strives to obtain *Uli* in prayer
Ia namu ia nawe   To mutterings, to pant for
                                 breath
Ka nehe i luna, ka nehe i lalo   The rustlings above, the
                                 rustlings below
Ka'a 'ākau, ka'a hema   Roll right, roll left.
Kū makani ha'i ka lani   The wind that splits the
                                 heavens,
Hekili ka'aka'a i ka lani   Thunder that rolls again
                                 and again
Kauila nui Mākēhā i ka lani   The great lightning that slashes
                                 in the heavens
Pane i ka lani e ola ke kanaka   Answer to the heavens,
                                 let the man live.
Hō mai ka loea, ka 'ike, ka mana   Bring cleverness, knowledge,
                                 supernatural powers
I a'e ka honua lā   So that earth may ascend
'O waha lau ali'i   By the mouth of many
                                 chiefs
'O kahi i waiho ai ka hua 'ōlelo   The place where words
                                 are left.
'Eli'eli kau mai   Profound is the *tabu*
                                 that rests upon it
'Āmama. Ua noa.   'Amama. It is free of *tabu*. [2]

The gods in turn passed on the power or *mana*
they represent to the people. Through the *mana*
one develops an awareness of unity and mutual
interrelationship of all that surrounds the individual.
The *mana* is passed on through a spoken declaration
or passed on by *hā*, a breath of life. *Mana* of the
prayer was in the word and names, but it was
also the breath that carried the words and names.

In the ritual of *hā*, a person's last breath is
passed with the giving of *mana* of a specific
talent or natural aptitude. Thus this power of
keen insight, understanding, and sensitivity
is given to chosen individuals to share and
pass on. The poetic vision and values are shared
through the breath.

This *hā*, the breath of life or breath of god, along with
alo meaning bosom or the center of the universe, forms
the word *aloha*. *Aloha* is the feeling and recognition of
the divine in everyone. *Aloha* is a view of life and a state of
mind and heart. The spirit of god,whichever form it takes, is in
everyone. Consequently, the understanding of *aloha*
necessitates the treating of everyone with reverence and
gentleness. Therefore, one cannot mistreat or judge another. We
each are given the responsibility of being a guiding light for one
another.

In the words of Pilahi Paki, "the *Aloha* Spirit is the coordination of
the mind and heart . . . it's within the individual--it brings you
down to yourself. You must think and emote good feelings to
others.

Permit me to offer a translation of the word *aloha:*
A stands for *akahai* meaning kindness,
          to be expressed with tenderness,
    L   stands for *lōkāhi* meaning unity,
               to be expressed with harmony,
        O   stands for *'olu'olu* meaning agreeable,
                    to be expressed with pleasantness,
            H   stands for *ha'aha'a* meaning humility,
                         to be expressed with modesty,
                A   stands for *ahonui* meaning patience,
                    to be expressed with
                      perseverance."[3]

Without *aloha* violence may follow.
In the Hawaiian tradition, one major cause
of violence is the loss of harmony within the self,
in relationships with others, and with the *'āina* (land).
Harmony is lost through lowered self-esteem, harbored
anger and hostility toward others, and the separation from
nature and the environment. More specifically, *Nānā I Ke
Kumu* [Look to the Source][4] explains the various causes for
violence:
personal vengeance resulting in loss of prestige, revenge for
mistreatment of a revered leader, boredom with peace, and
love of combat. The major cause of war and violence was
the dispute over possession of land that caused people
to kill.

However, to control the violence caused by war,
Hawaiians established ways to limit warfare. The most
effective was the *Makahiki* ceremony depicting the return
of the god *Lono* to Hawai'i. During the four month period
each year this was a time of festivals, harvest, taxes, games, and
sports. All warfare was halted. Other less effective control
measures to limit violence include periods of truce, total
abandonment of battle by mutual consent usually by
revelation of *hō'ailona* (omens), and *'ohana* relationships
(extended family) by chiefs realizing their family ties.

Another cause of violence is the oppression by
those in power and control. The oppressor
subjugates the values, way of life, and beliefs
of the powerless. This may take the form of
foreign invaders suppressing the land and its
people. Another form may be a subtle deculturation
process through an educational system which teaches
the perspective of the dominant culture. This form of
structural violence, serving the interests of the dominant
groups, demeans the subordinated individuals. The individuals
lose their dignity and self-worth which in turn generates further
hostility.

To arrive at nonviolence,
Hawaiians designed various activities to
maintain harmony for the individual and society.
In the cultural religious tradition, Hawaiians practiced nonviolence by channelling or neutralizing aggression and
violent forms of expression. They redirected energies
physically to release tension and provide time to play.

Ho'opāpā, an intellectual and poetic contest
of wits, was developed as a nonviolent form of battle.
Ho'opāpā takes the form of pitting one person's skills
against another by composing chants and riddles using
certain words, puns, and sounds. Skills required for
success went beyond logic to creative use of vast
storehouses of knowledge.

Another form of nonviolent activity is to focus positive energies
to fight common social ills such as environmental pollution and
nuclear disarmament. The social ill serves as a common bond
for the mass energy.

In addition, rules of proper etiquette to maintain
harmonious relationships were taught. Hawaiians
strongly believed in preventing violence by developing
nonviolent harmonious social behaviors. They were
careful in the words they used for fear of offending
or hurting someone's feelings.

The most important cause of nonviolence is *aloha*.
Aloha neutralizes violent actions and aggression. *Aloha*
within the *'ohana* from birth, childhood, and adulthood
provides positive reassurance and feelings of support for the
individual.

Nonviolence is developed and strengthened by living out the
spirituality that god is everywhere and in everyone. If god is
everywhere and in everyone, then we could not and would not
destroy or hurt anyone or anything around us.

Hawaiians of old attempted to treat others with much care for the spirit of god dwelling in all. In particular they generously shared their hospitality with all, including strangers. An old Hawaiian saying states, "'O Ke aloha Ke Kuleana o kahi malihini. Love is the host in strange lands."

Through this spiritual understanding that god is ever-present, the common overrides individual greed and gain. The welfare of others becomes more important than personal gratification. By realizing that one's survival and welfare are dependent upon a harmonious relation with other people and objects, one is led to harmonious actions and nonviolence.

To make the transition from violence to nonviolence in the Hawaiian spiritual tradition, individuals must feel loved and nurtured in an environment of acceptance and tolerance. The *'ohana*, or the extended family setting, provides a loving support to break away from violence. Through the giving of *aloha* in the *ohana*, the individual's violence may be transformed.

The nonviolent society as envisioned by Hawaiians, includes the following essential values integral to the Hawaiian spiritual tradition: a deep reverence and respect for all living objects

laulima   working cooperatively together for the good of the community

pono   justice, righteousness, and hope

lōkāhi   harmony in unity

ho'okipa   hospitality

lokomaika'i   generosity and goodwill

kōkua   mutual help and cooperation

'ohana   extended family, the sisterhood and brotherhood of humanity as central focus of relationships

aloha 'āina   love for the land,
understanding the
interdependence
of humanity and the
environment
mālama   caring for each other
aloha   the overriding value
of love and care for others.

These values need to be
articulated, taught, and nurtured
by all on this planet.

In addition to values to live by,
a nonviolent society needs to
practice a process of dealing
with problems and conflicts as they
arise. The Hawaiian process is
called *ho'oponopono*.

Ho'oponopono is a process of putting
things right with the whole person and god
and giving reverence to life. *Ho'oponopono*
is a process of forgiving each other. The
Hawaiians never parted still angry after a
disagreement. The families of both parties would
come together to work out the problem.

The individual must sincerely plead,
"Please forgive me in thought, word,
and deed if I have done anything to hurt you."
This begins the process. Some basic rules include:
keeping things simple by not being so entangled
and caught up in the words that one forgets the feelings,
forgiving at the forefront of the agenda, the need and desire
to be healed mentally and spiritually, getting right with god
releases the tension, pressures, and guilt, maintaining the
proper attitude, and believing in the power of prayer.

In *Nānā I Ke Kumu* Pukui describes the essentials of
ho'oponopono :

pule   opening *pule* or prayer as well as prayers at any
                later time when it seems necessary

kūkulu kumuhana   statement of the problem to be resolved

mahiki   the "setting to rights" of each
                         successive problem
                         self-scrutiny and discussion of
                         individual conduct, attitudes,
                         and emotions

'oia'i'o   quality of truthfulness
                                and sincerity
                                channel through
                                the leader
                                controls disruptive
                                emotions
                                leader questions
                                participants
                                honest confession
                                to god and each other
                                immediate restitution

mihi and *kala*   repenting, forgiving,
                           releasing from the guilts and grudges

closing *pule*
ho'omalu   period of silence to encourage
                  self-inquiry and calm tempers.[5]

On an individual level, we need to renew the
spiritual source of the Hawaiian religious and
cultural tradition to move toward a nonviolent
society. We need to live life with the understanding
of the relationship between the spirit of the people and
the spirit of the earth. There is spirituality and
physicality in all our actions and in who we are
in our daily lives. The sustenance for this life
comes from the land, water, and air. We need
to live this way of life in harmony with nature.

The environmental movement with its call to save
and care for the planet is raising the consciousness of the
people to the interconnection of all living things--to the
land, water, and air. It is calling for a simple lifestyle that
does not harm the earth. Environmentalists are reaffirming
what Hawaiian and other native peoples of the planet have
known all along. By caring for the land and the earth itself, we
come into harmony with what is around us.

On a public policy level, to move our society toward more
nonviolent conditions, we must provide an independent land
base for native people to practice and perpetuate their
culture and religious traditions. Without access to land,
particularly in a place like Hawai'i, violence is
created by denying the important spiritual link to the
land. Around the world, native people are claiming
their birthright to land as a cultural and spiritual link to
who they are. Nonviolent conditions may be created by
policy makers by allowing the native people rightful claim
to their land. Until this is done, cultural genocide and
oppression of these native people hang over each one
of us. For it is the native people of the planet, and
Hawaiians as a particular example, that culturally
have a spiritual tradition of nonviolence that can
serve as an example to others. This nonviolent
spiritual tradition calls for the harmony between
people, culture, and the environment.

Another recommendation for public policy
action for a more nonviolent society is the
creation of *pu'uhonua*, places of refuge.
Pu'uhonua are designated sacred areas
within which no blood can be shed nor
unkind word spoken. *Pu'uhonua* can
serve as zones of peace in areas of war
or provide shelter for those suffering
physical and psychological abuse--a place
of refuge for all to go for renewal and
protection.

NOTES

1. June Gutmanis, *Na Pule Kahiko* (Honolulu: Editions Limited, 1983), p. 2.
2. Ibid., pp. 113-114.
3. George Chaplin and Glenn D. Paige, eds., *Hawai'i 2000* (Honolulu: University of Hawaii Press, 1973), pp. 70-71.
4. Mary Kawena Pukui, E.W. Haertig, and Catherine A. Lee, *Nānā I Ke Kumu,* Vol. I (Honolulu: Hui Ha' Nai, Liliuokalani Trust, 1972), pp. 60-77.
5. Ibid.

Baha'i

Tony Pelle

Introduction

Baha'is are not strangers to violence. The persecutions of the Baha'i Faith in Iran, a Moslem nation, began as soon as the religion itself was born in 1844. The Bab (1819-1850), Prophet-Herald of the Faith and Forerunner of Baha'u'llah (1817-1892), Prophet-Founder of the Baha'i Faith, was martyred. In the early years of the Faith over 20,000 members were martyred. Baha'u'llah suffered persecution, imprisonment, banishment, and exile. Persecution of Baha'is continues intermittently to the present day. Baha'i holy places have been seized and in many cases destroyed. Elected officials of the Faith have been kidnapped and executed. Baha'is have been beaten, raped, terrorized and executed without trials. Cemeteries have been desecrated, private property looted and destroyed, life savings confiscated, and children expelled from schools. Again in Iran, Baha'is are officially considered non-persons and are deprived of their human rights.

Many governments of the world have appealed to Iran on behalf of the Baha'is and they have had some effect in reducing the severity and violence of the persecutions.

Why the persecutions? Why the violence directed against the Baha'is, particularly in the land of its birth? The Baha'i Community is the largest minority in Iran. Some of the reasons for the persecution are:

*Baha'is believe that Baha'u'llah is the Bearer of God's Word for this Age in the line of Abraham, Krishna, Moses, Buddha, Christ, and Muhammad. Baha'u'llah claims that all true religions come from the same Divine Source, that all the Prophets of God

13

proclaim the Word of God, and that religious truth is continuous and relative, not final and absolute.

*Baha'i teachings include the independent search for truth, abolishment of all prejudices, equality of men and women, harmony of science and religion, compulsory and universal education, abolishment of extremes of wealth and poverty, and a call for world unity and peace.

*The three basic principles of the Baha'i Faith are the oneness of God, the oneness of religion and the oneness of humankind.

All of these are seen as threats by Islamic fundamentalists.

How have Baha'is reacted to all the violence directed against them? They have responded with nonviolence. While obeying the government in all its laws and actions against them, the Baha'is made it clear that they remained steadfast to their Faith. The Baha'is of Iran, like the early Christian martyrs, have refused to recant their Faith, even when offered their lives in return for pro forma recantation of their Faith. They are firm in their love for their religious beliefs and have given up their lives for these beliefs.

What makes them withstand the violence directed against them and if need be willingly give up their lives for their beliefs?

Justice is a central concern of the Baha'i Faith and is seen as the expression of love and unity in the life of a society. Baha'is have accepted Baha'u'llah as the standard of justice for our age and the source of divine law. Baha'u'llah taught that a new world, a world civilization, can only be built by a new race of men and women whose actions reflect values of love, unity and justice that apply equally to all peoples.

Nonviolence and the Baha'i Faith

Baha'is completely reject the use of force to bring about a change in human affairs. They reject violence because it has its roots in lawlessness, it denies human rights due to all men, and it is contrary to moral law. Baha'is believe in the sanctity of all life. This includes nature which is to be respected and protected as a divine trust for which we are answerable.

Baha'u'llah states "Spread not disorder in the land, and shed not the blood of anyone."[1]

"Sanctify your ears from the idle talk of them that are the symbols of denial and the exponents of violence and anger."[2]

"Say: Fear God, O people and refrain from shedding the blood of anyone. Contend not with your neighbor, and be ye of them that do good. Beware that ye commit no disorders on the earth after it hath been well ordered and follow not the footsteps of them that are gone astray."[3]

"He [God] hath, moreover, ordained that His Cause be taught through the power of men's utterance and not through resort to violence."[4]

Abdu'l-Baha (1844-1921), son of Baha'u'llah who shared imprisonment with His father and visited the United States in 1912, states: "Fighting and the employment of force, even for the right cause, will not bring about good results, the oppressed who have right on their side must not take that right by force; . . . the evil will continue. Hearts must be changed."[5]

A Baha'i White Paper issued by the US Baha'i Community states: "We abhor killing and will never voluntarily place ourselves in a position where we must take human life."[6]

Baha'u'llah teaches that we should protect animals. "Look not upon the creatures of God except with the eye of kindliness and of mercy, for Our loving providence hath pervaded all created things and Our grace encompassed the earth and the heavens."[7]

"Shoghi Effendi (1896-1957, Guardian of the Baha'i Faith) links the preservation of the earth's resources with both the 'protection (of the) physical world and (the) heritage of future generations.'"[8]

Causes of Violence

The causes of violence are many and complex. They come from our experiences as individuals, as members of families, and as members of society.

"Aggression and violence are acquired behaviors which are neither innate nor inherited. (The exception is violence occurring under pathological medical conditions). They are the results of faulty views of the nature of man and the purpose of life."[9] How we view and understand good and evil, the purpose of life, threats and opportunities, attitudes about death and immortality affect our personal attitudes and are elements contributing to the amount of violence in the world today.

"A 10-year longitudinal study concluded that aggressive behavior is shaped by learning through socialization practices."[10]

"Observation by many social scientists indicate that one major cause of the ever-increasing presence and occurrence of violence and destruction in all societies is the discrepancy between the goals of the individual and those of his community."[11]

"Societies with a greater degree of competition, individualism and hierarchical structuring display a correspondingly greater amount of aggression and destructiveness. The competitive individual sets himself apart from his fellow men, thus causing division which can lead to aggression among the disunited lot."[12]

"Life without meaning results in despair, destruction, apathy and violence."[13]

Alan Watts states that man is violent because he identifies his real self with the ego--the ego which is continually striving against itself, society and nature.

Causes of Nonviolence

Why do people use nonviolence instead of violence? There are several reasons and the following are a few.

1. The religious and/or spiritual background of the individual: his or her moral value system.

2. Specific prohibitions in their religious or philosophical beliefs against violence.

3. The conscious decision of the person or the aversion of the person against violence.

4. The disgust of persons against acts of violence and their devastating results.

5. Nonviolence is part of the culture of the society in which the person is brought up.

Ruth Benedict sees aggression or violence in a society developing from the disharmony between an individual's objective and the wishes, norms and values of that society.[14] She states that "societies where non-aggressiveness is conspicuous have social orders in which the individual by the same act and at the same time serves his own advantage and that of the group."[15]

When the individual's and the community's objectives are in opposition many problems are caused for the individual including frustrations, fear and anxiety--all conducive to the development of aggression and violence.[16]

The teachings and beliefs of the Baha'i Faith negate violence and promote the use of nonviolence. The prime characteristic of the Baha'i community is unity.

"This unity is universal in nature and all-embracing in scope. It includes the development and safeguarding of love and harmony between the members of the community, as well as complete harmony and cooperation between those institutions of the Faith on the one hand, and between those institutions and the members of the community on the other."[17]

"This unity and love for each other among Baha'is is attained through the knowledge of God, so that men see the Divine Love reflected in the heart. Each sees in the other the Beauty of God reflected in the soul and finding this point of similarity, they are attracted to one another in love. . . . This love will bring the realization of true accord, the foundation of true unity."[18]

An important element in the Baha'i community is encouragement. Encouragement promotes the process of individual growth and creativity. First in this is the concept "that man is created noble, and that his innate nobility should be encouraged. Also important is the concept of the non-existence of evil."[19]

Violence is fostered by greed, prejudice or ignorance and self-centeredness. Nonviolence is fostered through concern for others, wanting to serve mankind, and love of truth and knowledge, all of which are promoted by Baha'i teachings.

Violence, as has been stated, is fostered by lack of concern and love for others. Abdu'l-Baha points to the example of fault-finding or back-biting and states "the most hateful characteristic of man is fault-finding."[20]

Causes of the Transition from Violence to Nonviolence

We previously quoted Watt's statement that man is violent because he identifies his real self with his ego. Some Baha'is have said the problem of ego and the part it plays in violence can be solved by adding a "w" to ego to get wego, suggesting that we must learn that as a civilization we have to see ourselves as part of the whole--instead of a separate "ego" we have "we go"--we go together.

Robert Muller, Assistant Secretary-General of the United Nations stated that "love is . . . the great transcending force which alone can break the nemesis of war and violence."[21]

Nonviolence is generally associated with protest action that negates something, for example, a protest against some particular system. But in actuality if nonviolence negates anything it negates violence. It attempts to lay building blocks for a new society where violence is illegitimate. This is positive nonviolence as opposed to non-violence. To do this we need nonviolent beings to build a nonviolent society. Violence is the product of the type of institutions and policies we follow.

Harlow Shapley, the noted astronomer, has suggested that rather than abolishing military forces we should use their abilities to organize and fight by redirecting their violence to a constructive use. He suggests we use them to organize and fight poverty, ignorance, senility and environmental problems.

Robert Muller states, "We must establish reverence for life as the cornerstone of civilization: reverence for life not only by individuals, but also by institutions, foremost among them nations."[22]

"The pivotal teaching of Baha'u'llah (Prophet-founder of the Baha'i Faith) is the oneness of mankind. The Baha'i Faith endeavors to create love at the individual and family level, unity at the community level, and peace in the international area of human relations."[23]

Characteristic Features of a Completely Nonviolent Society

"The Baha'i Faith sees man's life on this planet as only one phase in the ongoing progress of the human soul. Through this journey, which begins in the womb, the human spirit passes through all conditions of existence and acquires perfections or spiritual attributes such as knowledge, love, kindness, honesty, justice and so on."[24]

Baha'is believe in the immortality of the soul. Such a belief, it stands to reason, would also "eliminate or reduce those manifestations of violence which result from fear of nothingness or from frustration at the meaninglessness of life." [25]

Speaking of another Baha'i principle--the oneness of humankind, Shoghi Effendi states that it "implies an organic change in the structure of present-day society, a change such as the world has not yet experienced. . . . It calls for no less than the reconstruction and the demilitarization of the whole civilized world-- a world organically unified in all the essential aspects of its life, its political machinery, its spiritual aspirations, its trade and finance, its script and language, and yet infinite in diversity of the national characteristics of its federated units."[26]

"In the Baha'i Faith, the height of individual glory is expressed in service and humility."[27]

The worship and love of God is a point of unity among Baha'is worldwide. Abdu'l-Baha points out that "love is the greatest force in all of creation and the cause of progress, joy and everything that is constructive and conducive to human happiness and tranquility."[28]

There are several stages of love including love of self, marital love, etc. The abuse of love and power in human relationships "results in the development of fear, anxiety, anger, frustration and discouragement, all of which have been shown to be major contributors to the development of aggression and violence."[29]

What Should Be Done to Move Our Society Toward More Nonviolent Conditions?

We need to begin to build future nonviolent societies by starting with the education of the children. We need to include the following in their education.

1. Building a sense of love in our children. "Children tend to show their love by accepting the love given them by their parents."

2. The use of encouragement, i.e. "the focusing of attention on all that is good, positive, lofty and important in an individual." It is most important "that we educate our children about the nobility of their creation, the spiritual nature of their existence and the purposeful process of their lives. . . . Daily observations show that children who are subject to criticism and negative attention ultimately adopt those negative qualities. . . . Discouragement in any form impairs the development of the person's positive qualities. . . . Encouragement requires courage--the courage to be 'other-oriented' and not preoccupied with ourselves."[30]

3. Developing a proper understanding of the purpose and process of life. This decreases fear and anxiety in children and diminishes the development of resentment and violence.[31]

4. Building an understanding of our spiritual reality, the purpose of life and a sense of faith. "Such a way of life is integrated into the framework of the Baha'i Faith and its institutions, with their ultimate goal of establishing the unity of mankind and the prevention of violence and destruction."[32]

5. Developing a sense of faith in our children (and adults). "Faith is closely related to feelings of trust, which in turn help the individual to feel secure. . . . The capacity to trust enables the individual to depend on himself and others and to see signs of goodness in the whole of creation. . . . The capacity to trust and have faith begins at birth and is either encouraged or hindered throughout our lives. Those devoid of faith become suspicious, competitive, alienated, envious and prone to violence, suspecting the motives of others and doubting their own nobility, and that of the human race in general."[33]

6. Learning to deal with anger, aggression and violence in our lives. "We need to make a special effort to remove the cause of

anger and simultaneously avoid temptation to transform anger into aggressive and destructive behavior."[34]

7. Define the place of competition in our lives. "Competition has its roots in feelings of insecurity and self-doubt which adversely plague young individuals and societies alike. . . . An extremely important byproduct of competition is aggression and even violence."[35]

8. Learning cooperation. "A cooperative attitude is conducive to unity and freedom from violence."[36]

9. Working to develop a well-integrated personality in our children. "The development of faith, the improvement of one's ability to deal with anger, and the development of this capacity for cooperation are all extremely important undertakings which are made possible within the framework of interaction with others. . . . The manner in which a community deals with power and authority has profound effects on the ability of its individual members to become trustful and confident in their lives."[37]

Postscript

"The Baha'i Faith is not a political program for change--it is far more profound than that. It says that man can change himself, that he can climb to a higher stage in his evolution, leaving behind his former self, and entering a new stage in which his spiritual faculties, dormant until now, are more fully developed."[38]

Baha'is see man as possessing a spiritual and material nature. The new man, who is already in our midst, moves in the direction of the spiritual--love, mercy, kindness, truth and justice. The material aspect of man expresses untruth, cruelty and injustice. Baha'u'llah pictures the new man when He writes, "All men have been created to carry forward an ever-advancing civilization. . . . That one is indeed a man who today dedicates himself to the service of the entire human race." Baha'u'llah who suffered much persecution and was a prisoner for much of His life proclaimed: "The earth is but one country and mankind its citizens."

Baha'is are optimists. They see, through the grace of God, a better world in humankind's future. The prime movers in the change to a better world are the Prophets of God who have already come and who will come. They are the agents of man's spiritual evolution.

"To Shoghi Effendi, whose view of man was not in least utopian, we must turn for a final vision of what mankind, according to the Baha'i philosophy of history, has within reach:

> National rivalries, hatreds, and intrigues will cease, and racial animosity and prejudice will be replaced by racial amity, understanding and cooperation. The causes of religious strife will be permanently removed, economic barriers and restrictions will be completely abolished, and the inordinate distinction between classes will be obliterated. Destitution on the one hand, and gross accumulation of ownership on the other, will disappear. The enormous energy dissipated and wasted on war, whether economic or political, will be consecrated to such ends as will extend the range of human inventions and technical development, to the increase of the productivity of mankind, to the extermination of disease, to the extension of scientific research, to the raising of the standard of physical health, to the sharpening and refinement of the human brain, to the exploitation of the unused and unsuspected resources of the planet, to the prolongation of human life, and to the furtherance of any other agency that can stimulate the intellectual, the moral, and spiritual life of the entire human race.[39]

"All of the present communities of man, to varying degrees, promote violence and destructiveness. The political, economic, and religious systems need to undergo as fundamental a change in their premises and modes of functioning as do individuals in order to prevent violence. At the heart of these changes must be the realization that the community of man is an organic entity, and all people are its component parts. An injury to one is an injury to all. The unity of mankind is destined to become a reality once new institutions and concepts congruent with the oneness of mankind are widely established. Only then will our children be able to grow fully in a society free from violence."[40]

The Baha'i international governing body, the Universal House of Justice located at the World Center of the Faith on Mt. Carmel in the Holy Land, in its 1985 statement to the world, *The Promise of World Peace*, states: "The Great Peace towards which the people of good will throughout the centuries have inclined their hearts . . . is now at long last within the reach of nations. For the first time . . . it is possible for everyone to view the entire planet. World peace is not only possible but inevitable. It is the next stage in the evolution of the planet . . . 'the planetization of mankind.'"[41]

NOTES

1. Baha'u'llah, *Epistle to The Son of the Wolf* (Wilmette, Illinois: Baha'i Publishing Trust, 1979), p. 25.
2. Baha'u'llah, *Gleanings from the Writings of Baha'u'llah* (Wilmette, Illinois: Baha'i Publishing Trust, 1983), p. 73.
3. Ibid., p. 277.
4. Ibid., p. 278.
5. Abdu'l-Baha, *Abdu'l-Baha in London* (New York: The Baha'i Publishing Committee), p. 93.
6. (White Paper) *War, Government and Conscience in This Age of Transition* (Wilmette, Illinois: National Spiritual Assembly of the Baha'is of the United States, June 1969).
7. Baha'i International Community, *Baha'i Statement on Nature* (Office of Public Information, 1989).
8. The Universal House of Justice, *Conservation of the Earth's Resources* (Haifa, Israel: October 26, 1989).
9. Hossain Danesh, *The Violence Free Society: A Gift for Our Children* (Foreign Hill, Ontario: Canadian Association for Studies on the Baha'i Faith, October 1979), p. 38.
10. Ibid., p. 4.
11. Ibid., p. 8.
12. Ibid., p. 16.
13. Ibid., p. 31.

14. Ibid., p. 16.
15. Ibid., p. 16.
16. Ibid., p. 17.
17. Ibid., p. 17.
18. Abdu'l-Baha, *Paris Talks: Addresses Given By Abdu'l-Baha in Paris 1911-1912* (London: Baha'i Publishing Trust, 1969), pp. 169-181.
19. Hossain Danesh, op. cit., p. 20.
20. Abdu'l-Baha cited in *Canadian Baha'i News,* 1963. p. 7.
21. Robert Muller, *New Genesis* (Garden City, New York: Doubleday & Company, 1984), p. 73.
22. Ibid., p. 75.
23. Hossain Danesh, op. cit., p. 2.
24. Ibid., p. 6.
25. Ibid., pp. 12-13.
26. Ibid., p. 22.
27. Ibid., p. 24.
28. Ibid., p. 30.
29. Ibid., p. 33.
30. Ibid., p. 33.
31. Ibid., p. 33.
32. Ibid., p. 35.
33. Ibid., p. 35.
34. Ibid., pp. 36-37.
35. Ibid., p. 37.
36. Ibid., p. 37.
37. Ibid., p. 34.
38. Geoffrey Nash, *The Phoenix and The Ashes* (London: George Roland, 1984), p. 122.
39. Ibid., p. 122.
40. Hossain Danesh, op. cit., p. 38.
41. The Universal House of Justice, *The Promise of World Peace* (Haifa: Baha'i World Center, 1985), p. 1.

Buddhist *Robert Aitken*

I find the Buddhist rationale for social action to be grounded in the Four Noble Truths of the Buddha Shakyamuni:

1. Anguish is everywhere.

2. The source of anguish is our desire for permanence, and our desire to prove ourselves superior and exclusive. These desires conflict with the way things are: nothing abides, and everything and everyone depend upon everything and everyone else.

3. We find release from anguish with the personal acknowledgment and resolve: we are here together very briefly, so let us accept reality fully and take care of one another while we can.

4. This acknowledgement and resolve are realized by practice, and this practice, called the Eightfold Path, consists of Right Views, Right Thinking, Right Speech, Right Conduct, Right Livelihood, Right Effort, Right Recollection, and Right Meditation. Here "Right" means "correct" or "accurate"—in keeping with the reality of impermanence and interdependence. Here is my explication of the Eightfold Path:

1. Right Views offer a clear understanding that all things are insubstantial and transitory. They change and change again. Moreover, they completely depend upon each other. *This* is because *that* is; *this* happens because *that* happens.

2. Right Thinking is correct mental formulation of interdependence and the lack of any enduring self. It rests upon a mature, multi-centered attitude, rather than upon one that is self-centered. Right Thinking leads in turn to mature speech and conduct. For the responsible adult, Right Thinking is the careful use of temporary mental formulations that will be useful in persuading people what they know in their hearts to be true: that we

25

are here only temporarily, that countless generations will follow us, and that our fellow beings feel things every bit as keenly as we do.

3. Right Speech is the step on the path where we move from personal understanding to a position of active responsibility and leadership. When our words are in keeping with the true nature of things, then harmony and mutual support will be encouraged everywhere.

4. Right Action is logically the next step. Everyone is a teacher. By our manner and conduct we guide everyone and everything, for better or for worse. When we are settled and comfortable with our own transience and dependence, then our conduct in turn nurtures our sisters and brothers.

5. Right Livelihood is classically explained by showing how certain occupations create pain and confusion in the world: butchering, selling liquor, manufacturing weapons, trading in human beings, swindling, and so on. The rise of technology makes Right Livelihood difficult today. Few of us are crafts people with independent occupations. We must work for companies, very often large ones with questionable policies, or for a government, with its imperative of *Realpolitik*. Where should we draw the line, considering all the factors, particularly the support of a family?

Right Livelihood also implies fulfilling one's particular potential. This too is problematic today. Masses of people across the world are obliged to work in stultifying jobs, in circumstances at least comparable to the slavery which the Buddha deplored.

6. Right Effort is the way of the sage--an ultimately modest life style, traditionally with a simple diet of Earth products, and modest accommodations. This would include today the least wasteful means of transport.

7. Right Recollection is sometimes rendered Right Mindfulness. This is the act of consciously returning to Right Views, re-minding oneself to order thoughts and conduct in keeping with compassion. The parent or social leader at any level functions best with a wordless mantra, or perhaps even a mantra of words, as Gandhi did. Remember your source, and prompt yourself to recall it at each turn of your day. Soon this practice will be second nature, and you will come forth from your source with speech and conduct that can only be decent and loving.

8. Right Meditation refers not to simple reflection, but to "*samadhi*," a Sanskrit term that is translated in many ways, all of them flat or misleading or both. I think it is best to leave the word untranslated and just try to explain it. *Samadhi* is the practice and condition of a very settled, focused state exemplified by the seated images of the Buddha. As a perennial archetype it is the religious practice of an altogether sincere disciple of truth. Fulfillment of *samadhi* is the realization that the other is no other than myself--the personal inclusion of all beings.[1]

Many teachers succeeded the Buddha and mined his teaching for treasures that enrich it in turn. The *Hua-yen Sutra,* the last great development of Mahayana Buddhism, amplifies the Buddha's doctrine of interdependence with a multidimensional model of the universe called "the Net of Indra," in which each point of the Net is a jewel that perfectly reflects and contains all other jewels.[2]

The *Hua-yen Sutra* also offers the model of "the Tower of Maitreya" in its story of Sudhana, a pilgrim who studies under a succession of 53 great teachers. He learns much and deepens his practice until he meets Maitreya, the Future Buddha, the potential of every human being, and indeed of all beings. Maitreya leads him into his Tower, the ultimate abode of realization and compassion. When Sudhana enters, he finds the interior as vast and boundless as outer space, beautifully adorned with all manner of embellishments, and containing innumerable similar towers, each of them completely inclusive, infinitely spacious within, and likewise beautifully adorned, yet these towers do not in any way interfere with each other.[3] Thomas Cleary writes:

> This image symbolizes a central *Hua-yen* theme, represented
> time and again throughout the scripture--all things [are]
> interdependent, therefore imply in their individual being the
> simultaneous element of all other beings. Thus it is said that
> the existence of each element of the universe includes the
> existence of the whole universe and hence it is as extensive as
> the whole universe itself.[4]

Like the Buddha, the genius of the *Hua-yen* was not content simply to offer cognition of the truth of interdependence and interpenetration, but also required rigorous practice by way of application. The "Pure Conduct Chapter" of the *Hua-yen Sutra* consists entirely of *gathas*, cautionary verses that set forth explicitly the way of compassion that is grounded in the all-encompassing practice of one being as all beings. Here are some examples that set forth the way of the *bodhisattva* (those who enlighten themselves and others), translated by Thomas Cleary:

> When entering a hall,
> They should wish that all beings
> Ascend to the unexcelled sanctuary
> And rest there secure, unshakable.
>
> When on the road,
> They should wish that all beings
> Tread the pure realm of reality,
> Their minds without obstruction.
>
> If they see flowing water,
> They should wish that all beings
> Develop wholesome will
> And wash away the stains of delusion.[5]

Prompted by perceptions of trees, rivers, and other people-- by acts of entering the hall of a temple, stepping forth on a road, of dressing, brushing the teeth, going to the toilet--the student of the Way remembers to practice the all-encompassing views. Dr. Cleary uses the third person plural: "*They* should wish with all beings," but another translator working from the Chinese, where pronouns and prepositions are commonly omitted, might be more personal and render the line: "I vow with all beings." Thus the *gatha* about seeing flowing water could be:

> When I see flowing water,
> I vow with all beings
> to develop a wholesome will
> and wash away the stains of delusion.

I think that such a translation would be in keeping with a movement one can discern in Buddhism, and indeed in all religions, to make the teaching ever more personal and concrete. In the Far

East, this movement can be seen in the rise of the Mahayana, giving followers a sense of responsibility for the practice. For example, the Kamakura Reformation of twelth century Japan brought the recitation of the Buddha's name, and (to a lesser extent) Zen meditation to lay people. No longer was Buddhism just something for priests in the monastery.

This process of personalization and laicization can also be seen in the evolution of archetypal figures, such as Pu-tai and Kuan-yin, that give ordinary followers an intimate sense of involvement in the teachings of the Buddha and his successors. These figures are peculiarly Far Eastern, but are very instructive for us in the West.

Pu-tai, or Hotei in Japanese, is the ragged old monk in the tenth of the Ten Oxherding Pictures, who, in D.T. Suzuki's memorable words, "enters the city with bliss-bestowing hands."[6] After years of arduous practice, he has learned to forget himself completely, and so to embody compassion. He carries a bag filled with candy and toys for children, and mingles with publicans and prostitutes, leading them all to deepest understanding.

In China, the Pu-tai figure is inextricably mixed with Maitreya, the Future Buddha. Both are laughing figures with huge bellies. My teacher Yamamoto Gēmpo Rōshi used to say, "The whole universe is in Pu-tai's belly." It contains all beings, and he plays with them as richly diverse elements of himself. Thus he is also Maitreya Buddha, the fulfillment of our deepest aspirations.

Kuan-yin, or Kannon in Japanese, is called the Great Bodhisattva of Mercy and Compassion. Her name means "The One Who Hears Sounds." She is compassionate because she not only hears the innumerable sounds of suffering of the world, but she includes them. Like Whitman, Pu-tai, and Maitreya, she is large, and contains multitudes.

Pu-tai apparently originates in Chinese mythology, but Kuan-yin was first a male deity named Avalokiteshvara in the Indian Buddhist pantheon. He was the Sovereign Observer who dispensed mercy to those who petitioned him. He became androgynous and female in Far Eastern cultures, still dispensing mercy, as we can find in the *Lotus Sutra*.[7] From the Zen Buddhist point of view, at least, none of the archetypes of the Mahayana pantheon are exterior figures. They inspire us as our own noblest aspirations.

The process of making the religion personal and intimate for all followers continues as the religion moves to the West. Suddenly, Buddhism is taken seriously as a primary religion. This could not happen in the Far East. In China, Korea, and Japan, Buddhism has been secondary in importance to Confucianism, with its ideals of honor, loyalty to the superior, responsibility to the inferior, which set standards for human conduct. The Eightfold Path, the Buddhist Precepts, and the various myths and archetypes were, generally speaking, used simply as references and supplemental guides. In the West, Christianity and Judaism are the traditional religions, but Western Buddhists tend to move from those foundations and look to their new religion for counsel.

Thus the first vow of the Mahayana Buddhist, to save the many beings, can become as important for the Western Buddhist as the Lord's Prayer is for the Christian. Where does this vow extend? Does it apply to public affairs? The tradition that Buddhists should not become involved in politics should be seen clearly for what it is: simply a custom that grew up as a way of protecting the religion from persecution by Confucian and Shinto rulers. In the West we are not limited by such constraints, and our *dojo*, our place of practice and enlightenment, is as broad as the Earth, including everyone and everything.

So we plow new ground. The old ways are instructive, but they are exploded from their traditional confines. The Buddha Sangha or fellowship is still a network of relatively small groups of followers, but the followers are no longer necessarily priests, and no longer almost exclusively male. Looking over descriptions of self-governance within the traditional Sangha, we can pick up many ideas for community building among our own members,[8] but we can also pick up ideas from the Human Development movement in our modern culture.

Taking the Eightfold Path to heart, and making the Net of Indra, the Tower of Maitreya, the *gathas*, vows, and precepts our own, we find guidance in seeking harmony in our community, including our national and international community, and our inter-species community. We are free also to find inspiration from a vast pantheon of Western thinkers and doers, in particular those who have resisted the exploitations of big industry and the nation-state. E.F. Schumacher is an important teacher, as are earlier anarchist thinkers such as Peter Kropotkin and Gustav Landauer. Many cooperative movements, such as Liberation Theology with its Base Communities, the Catholic Worker, co-op groceries, investor-owned financial institutions, and land banks, show us what we can do and how we can go about it.

In the past, leaders of cooperative movements have made grave mistakes, and these can be instructive. In their anxiety to apply their ideals in the real world, such leaders sometimes neglected to establish firm ground for their structures, and saw them disappear. Most of the famous utopian communities in the nineteenth century, like Brook Farm, survived only a short time, some of them just a few months. The greatest utopian experiment of them all, the Paris Commune, lasted just seventy-two days.

Underlying these failures has been a serious underestimation of the massive power of conventional forces. Chief Executive Officers, Governors, and Senators might individually be concerned about the satisfaction of workers, peace in the world, and the protection of the environment, but they are at the mercy of systemic exploitation, even as you and I. Compromise with self-centered, corporate-centered, and state-centered enterprises are built into parliamentary procedures, and widespread despoliation of land, water, and air--and the extirpation of species--is the outcome. Earth and seas are dying, and the stockpiling of nuclear weapons makes hostages of us all.

What to do? The danger of the emergency should not blind us to the importance of what can be called the ninth step on the Path: Right Method. I am not sure just what this would be, but surely it involves first of all a life-commitment to perennial teachings, and to the kinship of all beings. As lay people we must resist destructive worldly conventions as vigorously as our clerical ancestors did in their hearts, if not in their deeds. And like them, we must find our home, our inspiration, and the support for our work with like-minded and like-spirited friends.

NOTES

1. Walpola Rahula, *What the Buddha Taught* (New York: Grove Press, 1974), pp.16-50.
2. Thomas Cleary, *Entry into the Inconceivable: An Introduction to Hua-yen Buddhism* (Honolulu: University of Hawaii Press, 1983), p. 37.
3. Thomas Cleary, *The Flower Ornament Scripture: A Translation of the Avatamsaka Sutra,* 3 vols. (Boston: Shambala, 1984-1987), III: 365-372.
4. Ibid., p. 7.
5. Thomas Cleary, *The Flower Adornment Scripture*, I: 316, 319, 321.
6. D.T. Suzuki, *Essays in Zen Buddhism: First Series* (York Beach, Maine: Weiser, 1985), p. 376 & plate X.
7. Bunno Kato et al., *The Threefold Lotus Sutra* (New York: Weatherhill, 1975), pp. 319-327.
8. Sukumar Dutt, *Buddhist Monks and Monasteries of India: Their History and Their Contribution to Indian Culture* (London: Allen & Unwin, 1962), pp. 66-91.

Christian *Stanley E. Amos*

You have heard it said, "You shall love your neighbor and hate your enemy." But I say to you, love your enemies and pray for those who persecute you.
Matthew 5:43-44.

Was nonviolence a term uttered by the members of the historic community of faith? Conceptually, "nonviolence" was non-existent. But pragmatically "nonviolence" was clearly visible in the lifestyle of the historic Christian community. There was historically as is contemporarily the need to juxtapose violence alongside nonviolence. We are now, as they were then, confronted with a choice--to participate in and/or support violence; to seek a neutral position; or to actively engage in nonviolence.

What is the underlying principle that helps us to determine our action and activity as Christians? What influenced the historic Christians of the apostolic church? Can the historic teachings regarding methods of responding to violence and of practicing nonviolence inform contemporary Christians or have the passing of centuries produced too tremendous a change for this to be fruitful? As contemporary Christians, what governs our actions and activities relative to nonviolence?

In an effort to address this series of queries, a proper starting place is essential. I must begin at the place that provides me with the strongest foundation on which to erect a sturdy and secure perception of nonviolence as it is viewed and practiced in the Christian community of which I am a part. The essence of the series of queries raised earlier is, "What is the basis for our commentary

33

and comportment regarding the concept and practice of nonviolence and its attending factors in contemporary times?"

The sure, sound, unchanging and unalterable foundation of the Holy Scripture is the proper starting place for our community of faith. Certainly the Christian community in its entirety varies in positions and perspectives regarding nonviolence.

It is therefore necessary to clarify that this is not an effort to argue against any particular perspective. It is rather an opportunity to put forth one Christian's perspective as it has been interpreted, defined, and practiced in the community of which I am a part. Therefore, I shall construct my perspective without delving into theological specifics.

Why does the Holy Scripture provide for us a basis for our acting and speaking on the issue of nonviolence? The Holy Scripture is unique as the Word of God. This above all else is the reason for the Scripture's authoritativeness. The Scripture contains the fundamentals of our faith which shape and color the specifics of our lives in the here and now as well as the hereafter. According to II Timothy 3:16, "All Scripture is given by inspiration of God, and is profitable for doctrine, for reproof, for correction, for instruction in righteousness." Not only is Scripture authoritative but its authority is comprised in the very meaning of the phrase "Holy Scripture."

Conclusively, the Holy Scripture has authoritative status within my faith community. Its authoritativeness demands that its status is never deemed irrelevant. The Scripture is always central and crucial. Therefore, the Holy Scripture does not demand our debates, or our considerations but rather our obedience to its precepts. This statement pertains to scriptural application and not scriptural interpretation.

Our responsibility is to be obedient to its teachings and to live its truths. As Christians in contemporary times, we are to enact its truths by removing them from the table of theory to the higher plane of practice. This is done when the Holy Scripture is read, studied, meditated on, lived, and witnessed. Such an application of methodology to this authority prevents members of this faith community from getting mixed up with the fads of the hour which might be logical but not godly. The Holy Scripture is essential to the interpretation and application by contemporary Christians of the concept and practice of nonviolence.

It is equally important to the Christian community to view the concept and practice of nonviolence from a Christological perspective. Jesus Christ is the supreme example for our faith community. Christ conveys to us the likeness of God. It is in Christ that we can understand better the order of divine love. It is Christ who has taught us the very principle of nonviolence. It is in Christ that we see the supreme demonstration of nonviolence.

The Sermon on the Mount, in which Christ shows the ability to love those who violently crucified him and to manifest that love by asking God the Father to forgive them, exemplifies specific teachings and actions that have and will continue to greatly influence the Christian community.

Loving concern for another rather than violence toward another has always been clearly evident in the ways of our Lord. Christ taught us in the parable of the Good Samaritan that we have an "obligation of making ourselves a neighbor to anyone in need." The fact of the matter is that people are affected by what we do or what we leave undone. Christ has taught us that sacrificial love is central, yet it is more than a feeling, it is also a commitment. An observance of the life of Christ, an emulation of that lifestyle, and an adherence to his teachings provide our community of faith a proper perspective regarding the concept and practice of nonviolence.

The Christian community is equally mindful of the activities of God in the Old Testament. In the Old Testament doctrines of creation and covenant, God is seen as the divine Person who creates man (humanity), breathing His spirit into him and molding him in His own image, and entering into an agreement with him that respects his freedom and integrity as a person. God purposed and possessed a desire for fellowship with humanity. His desire did not extend itself to the point of denying and disrespecting the freedom and integrity bestowed on humanity at the onset of his creation.

Throughout history there has been a perversion of this purpose. The perversion has produced estrangement between God and humanity. Many symptoms of this estrangement, too numerous to list in this writing, are clearly visible in our world today. Specifically so is the violent intentional destruction of another. Historically this was evident early on in the Cain and Abel episode.

Today we continue to experience the estrangement created by perversion of God's purpose and desire. Not only is there brokenness between God and man, there is brokenness between man and himself, man and other men, man and other groups of men. A great gap has been created. Christ came to gulf that gap.

In the first coming of Christ, among the many valuable lessons he taught, was the lesson legitimizing nonviolence. Says Christ, "Ye have heard that it hath been said, 'Thou shalt love thy neighbour and hate thine enemy.' But I say unto you, Love your enemies, bless them that curse you, do good to them that hate you, and pray for them which despitefully use you, and persecute you." Christ conveys to us that the continued employment of violence to address the issues of the present order is in reality the retention of the present order. And the present order as it is now is not what it ought to be. It must be transformed, not retained. It must be because we are not at that point where justice rolls on like a river and righteousness as a mighty stream.

Such teaching raises the questions, "Is there ever a right time to employ evil against evil, wrong against wrong, curses against curses, hate against hate, and violence against violence?" "Are we, as a community of Christ followers, to employ at all cost and times, good, right, blessings, and nonviolence as our way of life?"

The Scripture does not present us with an alternative, an option, or situational condition in which it is alright to employ evil for evil while remaining obedient to the teachings of our faith. There are specific methods for us to employ and they do not include the intentional effort to do harm to another.

Why are we taught to employ such methods? A basic look at the concept of violence juxtaposed alongside the will of God can help us to find an answer to this query. Violence connotes destructiveness. It is intrinsically evil when it goes against God's will and affects persons as well as the rest of God's creation. Violence carries with it an intentionality on the part of the victimizer to do harm to an opponent. Violence is degrading and corruptive.

Violence does not necessarily mean any act of disturbance. For Christians are called to disturb constantly those who create, inflict, and perpetuate conditions and situations of oppression, injustice, and other victimizations upon the creation of God in its totality. Christ disturbed the activities of those in the temple one day. His desire and intent was to bring a greater good as result of his act.

The definition of violence must be clarified. It is more than behavior designed to inflict physical injury or damage to property. If the definition were left there, we would have to seriously consider the surgeon and the bull-dozer operator. We must conclude that violence does not include all human aggression. Therefore, violence as used in the context of this writing is an intentional act done to another with the desire and/or goal to do harm without any intent of bringing out a greater good from the person as a result of the act. As it is used in the context of this writing, violence does not contain any healing value.

In recent times, one of the major proponents of nonviolence in our faith was Dr. Martin Luther King, Jr. Dr. King indicated that "violence . . . is both impractical and immoral. It is impractical because it is a descending spiral ending in destruction for all. The old law of an eye for an eye leaves everybody blind. It is immoral because it seeks to humiliate the opponent rather than win his understanding; it seeks to annihilate rather than to convert. Violence is immoral because it thrives on hatred rather than love. It destroys community and makes brotherhood impossible. It leaves society in monologue rather than in dialogue. Violence ends by defeating itself. It creates bitterness in the survivors and brutality in the destroyers."

Violence has the potential to destroy the semblance, essence and existence of community. God is not a God who desires to destroy community but rather to construct community. The potential of violence is antithetical to the will of God. The employment of violence prevents community whereas nonviolence makes it possible.

We are taught that upon our conversion, we are to reach out and strengthen our brothers and sisters, not destroy them (Luke 22:32). Our task is not to alienate and assassinate, but to strengthen and keep one another. The question raised by Cain, "Am I my brother's keeper?" must continually go forth from the lips of those who believe and trust the Word of God. Furthermore, the question must be answered with an emphatic and resounding "YES! I am my brother's keeper--not his assassin, but his life supporter--not his destroyer, but his keeper--not his downtrodder, but his uplifter."

Christians have a responsibility of leading others into the way that is good. Violence which intends to do harm to one's opponent does not permit that. Wisdom contained in the Scripture says, "A violent man enticeth his neighbour, and leadeth him into the way that is not good" (Proverbs 16:29). Violence does not allow us to arrive at the higher goal of harmony and unity among all people. While it is true that violence will achieve some goals, violence can never achieve the highest goal of love that exemplifies itself in unity and harmony among all humanity.

Certain periods in our history have given rise to a high spirit of contention. The Middle East crisis is a prime example. There are limitations to the technique and strategies that have been employed to grapple with the core of this crisis. What is certain is that when this act of war and violence is over, harmonious relationships with all involved will not be established because there is a limitation to what violence can achieve. The violence of war might force a militia to concede to your point of view, but it cannot create harmony and unity.

When the Middle East crisis comes to an end, if the currently employed strategies and techniques have not been changed, there will be distinctive divisiveness between the conqueror and the conquered, the strong and the weak, the haves and the have-nots, the developed and under-developed. Undoubtedly, there is some truth to the fact that violence may get you what you want. It has been demonstrated in the most recent past on the streets of Honolulu, on the streets of New York, on the streets of Gainsville, on the streets of South Africa. But--there is a distinct limitation to what will be accomplished when violence is employed as a means to arrive at an end.

One's demeanor is as important if not more important than his demand. The method employed to effect change is as important as the need to effect the change. Therefore the Christian must consider what it is that God ultimately wants to establish.

God ultimately wants to establish a new heaven and a new earth. The revelation of the new heaven and new earth is that of vanquished tears and death (Revelation 21:4). Violence is antithetical to the revelation because violence causes death and creates tears. Violence also creates and perpetuates chaos and confusion. We are convinced that "God is not the author of confusion, but of peace" (I Corinthians 14:33). Once we consider the divine desire of God, according to the received revelation, then it is incumbent upon the Christian community as instruments of God to press toward the establishment of a peaceful community by retaining the way of nonviolence and relinquishing the way of violence.

God is a God of reconciliation and not estrangement. Violence produces estrangement. It created brokenness and division between the aspects of God's creation. Violence denies reconciliation. Nonviolence helps to establish the right environment and climate for reconciliation. Our vision as a Christian people is that of a reconciled community.

Violence has the potential of disturbing your emotions to the point of clouding your vision. When the vision is clouded, the potential of missing the goal of harmony is maximized as a result of an imbalance in the emotions created by the act or thought of violence. The result is a desire to defeat which leads to wreckage rather than rectification.

Overcome by his emotions Peter committed an act of violence in the presence of Jesus. Jesus corrected both Peter and the violent act on the spot. Peter drew his knife and cut off a man's ear. Christ replaced the ear and rebuked Peter saying, "Put up again thy sword into his place: for all they that take the sword shall perish with the sword" (Matthew 26:52).

Violence does not liberate but rather imprisons. The Christian community is called to be a liberating force. In Luke, Jesus quotes from Scripture, "The Spirit of the Lord is upon me, because he has anointed me to preach good news to the poor. He has sent me to proclaim release to the captives and recovering of sight to the blind, to set at liberty those who are oppressed, to proclaim the acceptable year of the Lord" (Luke 4:18-19). Jesus is concerned about the victims and the liberation of victims. Violence is a victimizer and the jailer of its victims.

The Christian community is called to follow the way of nonviolence. Nonviolence is the principle and practice of doing no harm. Nonviolence is the active resistance to evil arising from internal strength manifesting itself externally in self-discipline. It provides one with the ability to love those who hate us. It is said truthfully that, "The power at the disposal of a nonviolent person is always greater than he would have if he were violent."

Nonviolence must begin internally with the great Christian value of love. It cannot begin externally with a practice that emanates from anything other than love. Neither cowardice nor passivity will suffice for these cannot truly transform relationships. Nonviolence transforms relationships.

In the Sermon on the Mount, Christ has prescribed a particular course of action for us. As Christians we are under obligation to follow this if we are to be the children of our Father in heaven.

Christ instructs us to do everything in our power not to let ourselves be caught up in the methods of our enemies. The Apostle Paul teaches us in Romans 12:21 that we are to overcome evil with good. The methodology of the enemy is never legitimate.

Situationists permit the use of violence depending upon the circumstances. When is it right to answer evil with evil? Such permissiveness is in violation of the teaching inherent in the book of Romans. In agreement with John C. Bennett, "there are particular patterns of activity that should be regarded wrong under all conditions."[1] Violence is that particular pattern of activity. There must be an outright rejection of answering evil with evil. Torture is less effective than mercy. Violence is less effective than nonviolence.

If peace is to be established and transformation is to take place, then we must accept the fact that there are certain essential conditions for peace. In agreement with Bennett, "we are called to care for the welfare and dignity of all neighbors, including enemies. We are called to seek for them justice and freedom."[2]

Such an attitude and action of care and concern is seen on a very small scale in our world today. Often the welfare and dignity of others is essentially nonexistent. Injustice seems to prevail in the streets, in the suites, and in the court system.

If there is to be peace, then there must be a transformation. There must be a transformation of our uncaring attitudes and behaviors such that love, care, and concern for the dignity and welfare of every person, regardless of race, creed, color, religion, and geographical location, becomes the order of the day locally and globally. If we are not careful, we will become the victims of our own self-righteous propaganda which will ultimately cost us our souls. That is too high a price to pay when the currently required wage is love.

It is said that "the whole Christian order is an expression of divine love." The Prophet Isaiah says in Isaiah 32:17, "And the work of righteousness shall be peace." "True peace is the fruit of love, since the divine order is the order of love. It is also a work of justice. Peace and justice have embraced each other. Love requires justice as its basis, its defence, and its witness."[3] This divine love must permeate and penetrate every human relationship. When this is done, violence must flee for it cannot exist in the same arena. Peace will reign supreme.

This imperative and radical transformation must not be dismissed easily as a religious shortcut or some solution of simplicity with great emotive but little to no practical value. If peace is to be realized, then this is a proper place to begin the realization. As Christians we are motivated, stimulated, and compelled by this religious imperative to seek and press continuously toward a peaceful order employing nonviolence as a means to the end. Following the instructions and perfect example of Jesus Christ will turn us in the right direction and will produce no limitations on our persistent and progressive march toward peace.

PEACE!

NOTES

1. John C. Bennett, *The Radical Imperative* (Philadelphia: Westminster Press, 1975), p. 48.
2. John C. Bennett, "The Issues of Peace: The Voice of Religion," a speech prepared for the Interfaith Conference on Religion and Peace.
3. P. Reganey, *Nonviolence and the Christian Conscience* (London: Parton, Longman, and Todd, 1966) p. 109.

Christian  *Anna McAnany*

Violence is the most urgent issue facing our world today. Institutionalized torture seems to be intensifying and ways of expressing it are becoming more cruel and refined. I ask myself the question, "Is violence natural or is it acquired?" Is it more prevalent in boys or in girls? In my family, I was the only girl with four brothers. I was always concerned when they got hurt in neighborhood fights. And when they were punished in school or at home, I felt the pain.

But, growing up in school, I responded wholeheartedly to the cry for victory to our army. I was thrilled with the strains of the Star Spangled Banner and the rockets red glare. And I say it with shame now that I was overjoyed when I heard that we had stopped the war in Japan with our powerful atom bomb. I just reasoned that now the war was over, we had won, and our men could come home now.

It was the Vietnam war that changed everything for me. I was taking classes at Notre Dame on the Prophets and I felt the impact of their message. I was to cry out against injustice, to take the side of the oppressed, and bring peace to the world.

I began to search the Scripture, to listen attentively to the message of God and to discover the strength of Christ. His was a message of peace and not a sweet passive peace but a strong call to justice for all. The Jews had expected a martial Messiah, one who would bring victory to their armies and abundance to their land. There was a tradition also of the Suffering Servant, but that was not encouraged as much as was the hope of a great kingdom.

It was Christ who fulfilled the promise of the Suffering Servant. In the garden, threatened with arrest, one of His disciples attempted to save Him by drawing a sword and cutting off the ear of His opponent. But Christ shielded him with these words: "Simon put away your sword. All who take the sword shall perish by it" (Matthew 26:52).

Being truly human, He was tempted to build His power kingdom with abundant riches and with the praise and flattery of human esteem. But He resisted that and made it clear that His power came from His Father.

Mahatma Gandhi, a non-Christian, was inspired by Christ's teaching and believed it was possible to save a whole nation from slavery to the British. He took seriously what Christ taught in His Sermon on the Mount. "Love your enemies. Do good to those who hate you. Pray for those who calumniate you" (Matthew 5:44). He preached the message of Christ with his life, not just with his words. And he was able to move an entire nation.

But Christ seems such a contradiction to our American way of life. Instead of retaliation, Jesus called for a loving response that would even submit to greater damage and suffering, rather than demand equal pain. Christ has said, "If a man would take your coat, give him your cloak also" (Matthew 5:40). And Gandhi would interpret this as "the greater the inhumanity, the greater the Power of suffering love necessary to begin restoring the bonds of community." Does this make sense to us? It was a most powerful force for victory in India.

Jesus revealed so profound a union between Himself and humanity that the crucifixion cannot be seen apart from a single injustice in history nor can it be separated from the personal confrontation of victim and executioner in any single injustice.

Christ was condemned to crucifixion by the Romans on the charge that He was a Zealot--a Jew committed to the violent overthrow of the Roman government. He was strongly tempted to join the Zealots, but He rejected it as satanic. Strange to say, when the power of Jesus took its outward form of weakness at the cross, His brave Zealots deserted Him. Rome had to confess it could not overcome the Cross. Rome's power was defeated by the strength of the empty tomb. Christ was able to transcend the state. He proved Himself to be free, but did not claim to be a freedom fighter. When challenged by Pilate, "Are you a king?" He responded, "My kingdom does not come from this world. I am a king. For this I was born and for this I have come into the world, to bear witness to the truth. Everyone who is on the side of truth hears my voice" (John 18: 36-37). Christ was not overcome by principalities and powers, mere earthly structures. Rather He made a public example of them, triumphing over them. He declared that love is the fulfilling of the law.

In the book of Revelation Christ is shown on a white horse, riding triumphantly (Revelation 19:11, 13). But He is also portrayed clad in a robe dipped in blood.

In the first centuries of Christianity, one had to renounce the military before he could be accepted into the Christian community. Because the military worshiped the emperor as their God, it was considered blasphemous to be part of it. But after Constantine became a Christian, he established a Christian empire. And to build up this empire he sent knights on the Crusades to restore power to the church. In their zeal to do this, they planted three crosses as a symbol of their power. But the force of these crusaders paled before the simplicity and poverty of Francis of Assisi. Long before the Green movement, Francis had realized the harmony and unity in all creation. In joy and freedom he saluted Brother Sun and Sister Moon. He had power over the wild animals and was able to communicate with them. He taught the people to trust and not to be afraid. He shared his meals with robbers who threatened him and tried to make friends with all. He went on the Crusades, not as a mighty warrior but as a friend offering love and trust. He succeeded where the knights failed. Thus he won the hearts of his enemies. The official teachings of the church supported peace, but also allowed for military enlistment.

St. Augustine had developed the conditions for a just war and these were accepted by the church until Vatican II. With the invention of the atom bomb, these conditions could no longer be acceptable, because no one could guarantee that only military targets would be reached.

Pacem in Terris was written by John XXIII in 1963. He emphasized that the fact that one is a citizen of a particular state does not detract from membership in the world community and common ties with all. He stressed the need for mutual trust among all nations. "Nothing is lost by peace; everything may be lost by war." He also stated that no country may unjustly oppress others or unduly meddle in their affairs. (Does this apply to the United States and Panama?)

Not every Catholic has been willing to follow the church's teaching on nonviolence. In fact in the United States many men felt called to defend their country by taking up arms. They have been persuaded that it is a patriotic duty to do so. We have even had members of the church hierarchy who supported the military and achieved high rank in it.

The American Bishops' *Pastoral on Peace* was a big step forward. It strongly condemned nuclear war but it hesitated to pronounce anything on deterrence. And even this pastoral has not received the attention it deserves nor the implementation it needs.

However there have been many courageous witnesses to peace today. In World War II, we had Ben Salmon who conscientiously resisted military service and was crucified mentally and physically for his refusal to join the military. He was even incarcerated in a mental hospital, in hopes that this would break him. He was misunderstood by his family, his country and even his church.

And in Austria there was the solitary witness Franz Jägerstätter, a Catholic man, who refused to serve under Hitler and was rejected by his church, his family, and his country for doing so. Christ alone was his support when the Nazis beheaded him in Berlin in 1943.

One who has had a great influence on war resistors was Dorothy Day who declared that the purpose of civil disobedience is to make clear the injustice of the law so that even the perpetrator of the injustice will come to admit the fact and be willing to change. Such a person is strong and has great power to open the eyes of the oppressor to new values. She is seeking the openness of free exchange to which reason and love have freedom of action.

Thomas Merton, a contemplative monk, has said that the American mind is largely negative and has a completely inadequate image of nonviolence. But we must refuse to despair of the world. We need to prefer love and trust to hate and suspicion. Christian nonviolence cannot encourage or excuse hatred of a special class or color. It must be built on the basic unity of the human family, searching for the truth common to them *and* their enemy.

Pope Paul VI said: "While so many people are going hungry, while so many families are suffering destitution, while so many people spend their lives submerged in the darkness of ignorance, while so many schools, hospitals, homes worthy of the name, are needed, every public or private squandering . . . every financially depleting arms race . . . all these we say become a scandalous and intolerable crime. The most serious obligation enjoined on us demands that we openly denounce it."

The popes of the last seven decades have never tired of calling for a world order of peace. Today we know more than ever how important it is to have a world order of peace. In a world where everything and everybody is interrelated on a hitherto unknown scale, it has become an urgent ethical commandment.

As a Christian I believe that Jesus Christ is the incarnation of the only true God who is *Agape,* unconditional love, unending forgiveness and merciful love. It is the spirit of this God that is life giving. It is this God in whose image and likeness we are all formed.

Therefore we need to say clearly, again and again, that violence is not the Christian way, nor the Catholic way, nor the way shown by Jesus.

The Christian faith upholds the sacredness of life, of all life. It demands a reverence for the mystery of life in plant, and animal, and human life, both male and female. It teaches that we are created for unity; that we are called to empower each other. It acknowledges sin as that which separates us, leads us to try to surpass one another, and eventually to destroy the other, simultaneously destroying ourselves as well. Our task in life is to restore the unity of the human family and to share the fruits of the earth with one another.

Christ has reduced the whole law to two commandments. Love the Lord your God with your whole being; and love your neighbor as yourself. And very specifically he says, "Thou shalt not kill." This must be heeded not just in personal dimensions, but also in its collective dimensions such as the state capital punishment and war. We legitimize killing when the state carries it out. We put nationalism before our common humanity. Flags have destroyed many people. We are all children of God. We Christians must admit we have betrayed our leader Christ. We have modified the teachings of Christ and made them conform to our standards. We need to give full attention to the gospel of peace and nonviolence.

In Nicaragua, Tomas Borge, who had been imprisoned and tortured by the national guard, had to stand by and watch his pregnant wife Yelba savagely raped, tortured and killed. This man as minister of the interior after the Sandinista victory over Samoza confronted his wife's murderer with these words: "My revenge will be to pardon you." As Nicaragua's new minister of the interior he eliminated capital punishment and torture. The Sandinista government has a deep commitment to the sanctity of human life.

Even in a so-called "just war," violence is evil. No one really wins. As John Paul II says: "Wars not only destroy human life, but also damage the land, ruining crops and vegetables as well as poisoning soil and water. The survivors of war are forced to begin a new life in very difficult environmental conditions which in turn create situations of extreme social unrest, with further negative consequences for the environment."

How is our human nature evolving? Are we becoming more compassionate, more understanding, more spiritual? Or are we willing to destroy, to hurt, to kill? If we descend to this level, we will destroy this planet, our human family, and our own personality. Christians have never questioned the teachings on nonviolence. They have just declared they do not want to live by them. We have been more loyal to our nation than to our God. We have approved of capital punishment and we have been eager to profess our love for country and to kill for it. As we dilute our sacred values, we also diminish ourselves and our country. And while we kill others, we also commit our loved ones to be killed. In recent years a number of Catholics have witnessed to nonviolence at the sacrifice of family, friends, freedom and even life itself.

The Church today is raising up examples of heroic people who are willing to be imprisoned so that others may be free--to die so that others may live: Dan and Philip Berrigan, Elizabeth McAllister, Dorothy Day, Thomas Merton, Jim Douglass and Ben Salmon are just a few of these people.

Here are some Christian statements on nonviolence.

"Love your enemies and pray for them that persecute you. If you love those that love you, what reward will you have?" (Matthew 5: 43-44).

"Do not resist one who is evil, but if anyone strikes you on the right cheek, turn to him the other also" (Matthew 5: 39-40).

"Love is patient and kind, love is not jealous or boastful. It is not arrogant or rude. Love does not insist on its own way" (1 Corinthians 13: 4-6).

"Peace demands the most heroic labor and the most difficult sacrifice. It demands greater heroism than war. It demands greater fidelity to the truth and a much more perfect purity of conscience" (Thomas Merton).

"Injustice anywhere is a threat to justice everywhere. I have been so greatly disappointed with the white church and its leadership" (Martin Luther King, Jr.).

"O Lord, make me an instrument of your peace, where there is hatred . . . let me sow love, where there is injury . . . pardon, where there is darkness . . . light, where there is sadness . . . joy, where there is doubt . . . faith, where there is despair . . . hope. O Master, grant that I may not so much seek to be consoled . . . as to console, to be understood . . . as to understand, to be loved . . . as to love, for it is in giving that we receive, it is in forgiving that we are pardoned, and it is in dying that we are born to eternal life" (Prayer of St. Francis Assisi).

"Vengeance is mine; I will repay. If thine enemy hunger, feed him; if he thirst, give him drink, for in so doing, thou shalt heap coals of fire on his head. Be not overcome by evil, but overcome with good" (Romans 12:20-21).

"Peace is an equilibrium that is based on motion and continually gives forth energy of peace and action; it is intelligent and living courage" (Paul VI, 1978).

"Happy are those who know they are spiritually poor; the kingdom of heaven belongs to them! Happy are those who are merciful to others; God will be merciful to them! Happy are those who work for peace; God will call them His children! Happy are those who are persecuted because they do what God requires; the kingdom of heaven belongs to them! Happy are you when people insult you and persecute you and tell all kinds of evil lies against you because you are my followers. Be happy and glad, for a great reward is kept for you in heaven" (Matthew 5: 3-11).

Hindu  *Gurudeva Sivaya Subramuniyaswami*

Ahimsa is the highest dharma.
It is the highest purification.
It is also the highest truth
From which all dharma proceeds.
Mahabharata (XVIII: 1125.25).

Querist: What are the sources of Hindu thought which inspire men to live the ideals of compassion and nonviolence?

Gurudeva: The *rishis* who revealed the principles of *dharma* or divine law in Hindu scripture knew full well the potential for human suffering and the path which could avert it. To them one spiritual power flowed in and through all things in this universe, animate and inanimate, conferring existence by its presence. To them life was a coherent process of maturity leading all souls without exception to enlightenment, and no violence could be carried to the higher reaches of that ascent.

These *rishis* were mystics whose revelation disclosed a cosmos in which all beings exist in mutual dependence. The whole was contained in the part, and the part in the whole. Based on this cognition, they taught a philosophy of non-difference of self and other, asserting that in the final analysis we are not separate from the world and its manifest forms nor from the Divine which shines forth in all things and all peoples. From this understanding of oneness arose the philosophical basis for the practice on non-injury and Hinduism's ancient commitment to it.

We all know that Hindus, who are one sixth of the human race today, believe in the existence of God everywhere, as an all-pervasive, self-effulgent energy and consciousness. This basic belief created the attitude of sublime tolerance and acceptance toward others. Even tolerance is insufficient to describe the compassion and reverence the Hindu holds for the intrinsic sacredness of all

49

things. Therefore, the actions of all Hindus are rendered benign or *ahimsa*. One would not want to hurt something which one revered. On the other hand, when the fundamentalists of any religion teach an unrelenting duality based on good and evil, man and nature, or God and Devil, this creates friends and enemies. This belief is a sacrilege to Hindus because they know that the attitudes which are the byproduct are totally dualistic, and for good to triumph over that which is alien or evil, it must kill out that which is considered to be evil.

The Hindu looks at nothing as intrinsically evil. To him the ground is sacred. The sky is sacred. The sun is sacred. His wife is a goddess. Her husband is a god. Their children are *devas*. Their home is a shrine. Life is a pilgrimage to *mukti* or liberation from rebirth, once attained never to reincarnate in a physical body. When on a holy pilgrimage, one would not want to hurt anyone along the way, knowing full well the experiences on this path are one's own creation, though maybe acted out through others.

Querist: How does Hinduism define *ahimsa* ?
Gurudeva: In Sanskrit *himsa* is doing harm or causing injury. The "a" placed before the word negates it. Very simply, *ahimsa* is abstaining from causing hurt or harm physically, mentally, or emotionally. It is gentleness and non-injury. It is good to understand that non-violence (as opposed to nonviolence) speaks only to the most extreme forms of wrongdoing, in contrast to *ahimsa* which goes much deeper, to the subtle abuse and the simple hurt.

In his commentary on the *Yoga Sutras*, sage Vyasa defines *ahimsa* as "the absence of injuriousness (*anabhidroha*) toward all living beings (*sarvabhuta*) in all respects (*sarvatha*) and for all times (*sarvada*)." He noted that a person who draws near one engaged in the true practice of *ahimsa* would be freed from all enmity. Similarly, Patanjali (*circa* 100 CE) regards *ahimsa* as the yogi's *mahavrata*, the great vow and foremost spiritual discipline which those seeking Truth must follow strictly and without fail. This was not meant to merely condemn killing, but extended to harm caused by one's thoughts, words and deeds of all kinds--including injury to the natural environment. Even the intent to injure or violence committed in a dream is a violation of the principle of *ahimsa.*

Querist: Can you please give a summary on how beliefs, attitudes and actions interact to produce peace or violence?
Gurudeva: The *Brihadaranyaka Upanishad* (IV, 4, ii, 6) says: "Here they say that a person consists of desires. And as is his desire, so is his will. And as is his will, so is his deed; and whatever deed he does, that he will reap." Every belief creates certain attitudes. Those attitudes govern all of our actions. Man's actions can thus be traced to his inmost beliefs about himself and about the world around him. If those beliefs are erroneous, his actions will not be in tune with the universal *dharma.* For instance, the belief in the existence of an all-pervasive Divinity throughout the universe creates an attitude of reverence, benevolence and compassion for all animate and inanimate beings. This equals *ahimsa,* non-hurtfulness. The belief in the duality of heaven and hell, the white forces and the dark forces, creates the attitude that we must be on our guard, and that we are justified in giving injury, physically and emotionally, to others whom we judge to be bad, pagan or unworthy for other reasons. We can sum this up from the Hindu/Buddhist tradition: *ahimsa* is higher consciousness, and *himsa,* hurtfulness, is lower consciousness.

Querist: What are the reasons that most Hindus oppose killing?
Gurudeva: Belief in *karma* and reincarnation are strong forces at work in the Hindu mind. They know full well that any thought, feeling or action sent out from themselves to another will return to them through yet another in equal or amplified velocity. What we have done to others will be done to us, if not in this life then in another. The Hindu is thoroughly convinced that violence which he commits will return to him by a cosmic process that is unerring. Two thousand years ago South India's weaver saint Tiruvalluvar said it so simply, "All suffering recoils on the wrongdoer himself. Therefore, those who desire not to suffer refrain from causing others pain." A similar perception can be found in the Jain scripture *Acaranga Sutra:*

To do harm to others is to do harm to oneself. You are he
whom you intend to kill. You are he whom you intend to
dominate. We corrupt ourselves as soon as we intend to
corrupt others. We kill ourselves as soon as we intend to kill
others.

Ahimsa is certainly not cowardice; it is wisdom. And wisdom is
the cumulative knowledge of the existing divine laws of
reincarnation, karma, *dharma,* the all-pervasiveness and sacredness
of all things, blended together within the psyche or soul of the
Hindu.

Querist: What are the causes of transition from violence to
nonviolence? Why have some Hindus changed from approval of
killing to opposition to it? In short, how do we move from violence
to nonviolence?

Gurudeva: There are millions of Hindus who are born into the
Hindu religion because their parents and forefathers profess that
faith, but who are not educated in the Hindu beliefs which will
produce proper attitudes. Because they are Hindus, their desire to
pursue the depth of their religion wells up, often in later life.
Through soul-searching, self-examination and psychological
overhaul--not without a lot of mental pain attached--the old beliefs
are replaced with the new. A conversion has taken place within the
subconscious mind. The computer program within the *muladhara
chakra* has been updated. Through this process, the meat-eater
becomes a vegetarian, a hurtful person becomes kindly, *himsa*
becomes *ahimsa.*

Querist: Can you say something about how peace is a reflection of
spiritual consciousness, and violence a reflection of unevolved or
base consciousness?

Gurudeva: The Hindu knows that at this time on the planet those
of the lower nature, unevolved people, are society's antagonists.
Being unevolved, they are of the lower nature, self-assertive,
confused and protective of their immediate environment. All others
are their enemies. They are jealous, angry, and fearful. Many take
sport in killing for the sake of killing, thieving for the sake of theft,

even if they do not need or use the spoils. This is the lower nature, and is equally distributed among the peoples of the world, every nation and society. Those of the higher nature--10, 15 or 20 percent of the population--live in protective environments. Their occupation is research, memory, education, which is reason; moving the world's goods here and there, which is will. Those of yet a higher nature delve into the mysteries of the universe, and others work for universal peace and love on earth, as groups and individuals. The Hindu knows that those of the lower nature will slowly, over an experiential period of time, come into the higher nature, and that those of the higher nature, who have worked so hard to get there, will avoid the lower nature and not allow themselves to be caught up into it. Hindus believe in the progress of humanity, from an old age into a new age, from darkness into a consciousness of divine light.

Querist: You have said before there is a spiritual urge in every soul for peace, that even if a person is violent now, he or she inwardly yearns for peace. Is that so?

Gurudeva: Man is essentially an instinctive, intellectual and superconscious, or soul, person. The instinctive nature is based on good and bad, mine and yours, up and down pairs of opposites. The soul nature is based on oneness, humility, peace, compassion, love, helpfulness. The intellectual nature is based on trying to figure both of these two out. It juggles knowledge from the lower nature to the higher nature and from higher nature to the lower nature. It works out formulas, finds solutions and processes knowledge. The key is *yoga*, yoking the soul with the energies of the physical body (the instinctive nature) and yoking the energies of the soul with the energies of the mind (intellectual nature) and then, simply, one becomes consciously conscious in the soul. This is an experience to be experienced, and for the Hindu it is personal experience of God which is essential for liberation. The Hindu strives to be consciously conscious of his soul. When those soulful qualities are unfolded, he is filled with a divine love and would not hurt a flea if he could help it.

Querist: What's the best way to teach peace to the world?
Gurudeva: The best way is to teach families to be peaceful within their own home, to settle all arguments and contention before they sleep at night, even if they stay up for three days, so the children can see that peace can be attained and then maintained through the use of intelligence. Humans do not have horns or claws, nor do they have sharp teeth. Their weapon is their intelligence. Children must be taught through the example of parents and by learning the undeniable facts of life, the basic tenets--that an all-pervasive force holds this universe together, that we create with this force every minute, every hour, every day, and because time is a cycle, what we create comes back to us. Therefore, because we create in a physical universe while in a physical body, we must return to a physical body, in a new life after death, to face up to our creations, good, bad or mixed. Once children learn this, they are winners. It is up to the parent to create the peacemakers of the future. It is always up to the parent. And remember, we teach children in only one way--by our own example.

Parents must teach children to appreciate those who are different, those who believe differently. Teach them the openness that they need to live in a pluralistic world where others have their way, their life and culture. Teach them the value of human diversity and the narrow-mindedness of a provincial outlook. Give them the tools to live in a world of differences without feeling threatened, without forcing their ways or their will on others. Teach them that it never helps to hurt another of our brothers or sisters.

Querist: Why or how does Hindu philosophy contain the seeds of peace? Is it because of the belief in reincarnation? Because one knows that he may be in the same position of the one he might be inclined to harm or persecute?
Gurudeva: This is true. The Hindu who is consciously aware within his soul knows that he is the time traveller and may incarnate, take a body of flesh in the society he most opposed in order to equalize his hates and fears into a greater understanding which would result in the release of ignorance. The knowledgeable Hindu

is well aware of all these possibilities. The mystery is no mystery to the mystic.

Querist: Is it possible for the individual, the society or the global community to be completely nonviolent?

Gurudeva: When the injustice of killing happens no more, then and only then will the next *yuga* or human epoch commence in its fullness. The farseeing *rishis* of our religion have predicted what we see today. So today is no worry to us. But the Hindu is bound by his intelligence to pass along to the next generation methods of improvement pointing out the errors made in the past and outlining better directions for the future. A Hindu's method of saving the world is lifting up each individual within it.

Definitely, an individual can find total peace within himself, not through meditation alone, not through drugs, not through psychology or psychiatry, but through control. Peace is the natural state of the mind. It is there, inside, to be discovered and then radiated out to others.

Querist: How do we bring individuals to this point?

Gurudeva: Let them go for one year without experiencing confusion in their thinking, covetousness of another's goods, the wish to kill to solve a problem, and anger, jealousy or fear. After that year, they will be a very peaceful person. This is because of the soul knowledge they will have gained in overcoming these instinctive forces which will release their consciousness to a natural state of peace.

Querist: Can a community or society be totally nonviolent?

Gurudeva: Well, of course, if the educational system promotes it, in every community the greatest potential for peace will be achieved. The educational system is controlled by the adults, so they have to come to terms with two facts. First, that they must not be hurtful-- physically, mentally or emotionally. Second, they must understand the basic principles of the *sanatana dharma*: all-pervasive energy, cause and effect, and coming back in a physical birth until all scores are settled. Once the adults accomplish this, these basic principles of life will be passed on to the next generation.

Querist: What about the fact that some are always coming up through the instinctive nature, and thus even though mature souls have achieved peace, others are coming along the path?

Gurudeva: This is true. In a complete humanity, there are always those of higher consciousness and those of lower consciousness. At this time on the planet, it is the intrinsic duty of higher-consciousness people to be more self-assertive, let their voices be heard and take up the banner in a heroic way, join committees, enter government, while at the same time maintaining the peace within their own home and holding a benign reverence for all living beings.

As the vibration of the planet earth changes, the mood of the people will change. *Ahimsa* begins in the home, in the bedroom, in the kitchen, in the garden, in the living room. When *himsa*, harmfulness, arises in the home, it must be settled before sleep, or else those *vrittis*, those waves of the mind, which were disturbed by the creation of the situation, will go to seed to erupt at a later time in life. We cannot expect the children to control themselves if the parents do not control themselves.

Those who attain a personal peace by controlling their instinctive nature become the spiritual leaders of human society. People who do become these leaders retroactively control the masses because of their spirit, their soul force--not because of mind force, their cleverness, their deceptions, their political force, their money or contacts. They are the people in the higher consciousness who control lower consciousness, by lifting up the masses, as parents are supposed to uplift their children.

Querist: What would it take, according to Hinduism, in the way of change, to have a nonviolent world?

Gurdeva: It would simply mean that all individuals have to somehow or other reconcile their differences enough so that the stress their differences produce can no longer take over their mind, body, and emotions, causing them to perform acts of violence. Again, this would begin in the home. Peaceful homes would breed gentle people. Gentle people are *ahimsa*. Furthermore, the belief structure of each individual must allow for the acceptance of the eternal truths, which I mentioned before--returning to flesh to reabsorb back the karmic energies released in a previous life, and of course, the belief in the existence of an all-pervading power. As long as our beliefs are dualistic, we will continue to generate antagonism and that will erupt here and there in violence.

At an international and national level, we must become more tolerant. Religious leaders and their congregations need to learn and teach tolerance for everyone and everything, for other faiths. First this must be taught to the religious leaders themselves, the rabbis, the *imams*, the *rōshis*, the *swamis* and priests. Tolerance and intolerance are basic attitudes found in our belief systems. These are things that one can learn.

In our various nations, in the United Nations and other world bodies we can promote laws which recognize and take action against crimes of violence. The world must as a body come to the conclusion that violence is totally unacceptable. To abhor violence is a state of higher consciousness.

Querist: What about on a personal level, what are some of the keys to finding peace in one's life?
Gurudeva: Vegetarianism is very important. In my forty years of ministry, it has become quite evident that vegetarian families have far less problems than those who are not vegetarian.

The abhorrence of killing of any kind leads quite naturally to a vegetarian diet. If you think about it, the meat-eater is participating in a violent act indirectly, toward the animal kingdom. His desire for meat drives another man to kill and provide that meat. The act of the butcher begins with the desire of the consumer. When his consciousness lifts and expands, he will abhor violence and not be able to even digest the meat, fish and eggs he was formerly eating. The opposite of causing injury to others is compassion and love for all beings. A great Hindu scripture puts it nicely: "How can he practice true compassion who eats the flesh of an animal to fatten his own flesh?"

If children are raised as vegetarians, every day they are exposed to nonviolence, as a principle of peace and compassion. Every day they are growing up, they are remembering and being reminded not to kill. They won't even kill another creature to eat, to feed themselves. And if you won't kill another creature to feed yourself, then when you grow up you will be much less likely to do acts of violence to people.

Querist: What is it that causes someone who was previously violent to become nonviolent?

Gurudeva: It is a matter of realizing what life is really all about and how violence violates our own inner being. When a violent act is committed, it makes a mark deep within the mind of the individual. The individual who becomes penitent brings higher energies into himself, and these energies slowly heal this mark. But there is more to it than this. Certain kinds of spiritual "therapy" must go along with the penitent mood for a total healing to occur, which would be absolution. This therapy is finding a way to pay back society for the harm caused in that act of violence. It may be working as a nurse's aid or as a volunteer to help in the healing of people who have been victimized by the violent acts of others. The modern laws of community service are good, but for a total healing and change of heart, the service to the community should be more directly related to the actual crime the person committed. Finally, over a long period of time, the matter is totally resolved in the mind of the person and those who know him. Then he would be as much a nonviolent as he was a violent person.

Querist: Is there a revelation or realization to bring someone who previously felt OK about violence to feel now not OK about it? One example that people are familiar with is the experience of the astronauts who orbit the earth. From their cosmic perspective they see no borders, no divisions, only a one small planet, and this has tended to make them peacemakers.

Gurudeva: This indeed would be a revelation of higher consciousness. In deep states such visions happen and do change peoples' lives. But contemplative experiences come for the most part to contemplative people, and if we are referring to meditation and yogic practices here, they should not be performed by angry people, jealous people, confused people, lest the uplifted energies plummet and intensify the anger and other aspects of the lower nature. The better way would be for the angry, violent person to become religious and consistently to do small religious acts. For these despicables will get their solace through remorse, repentance, reconciliation and finally absolution. Even the Gods do not penetrate the sunken depths in which they live.

Querist: But many people do have life-transforming mystical experiences--a soldier on a battlefield, someone who nearly dies. And they happen out of the blue. Can these transform?
Gurudeva: Definitely, but the point I was trying to make is that transforming experiences come to real nice people, people with love and trust. Maybe they are not too intelligent and get drawn into situations where they are overtaken by a fit of temper. But their remorse is immediate. Maybe the karma caused is heavy, but their soul goes to work on the situation and the healing process starts within their mind. Possibly the intensity of the violent mishap itself creates the big awakening, the big change, and catalyzes the change to higher consciousness.

Querist: There is the idea that by our own decisions and actions, in everything we do, we promote peace or we promote violence. What can we do as individuals or institutions responsibly to promote nonviolence?
Gurudeva: Make a list of all the things you have purchased in the last six months which bring harm to humans, animals, and even the environment. Read the labels on even simple things like glue or soap and scratch off the list all the things that contribute to violent acts or aid in the destruction of the planet. Then find the willpower not to fall back, for convenience sake, into purchasing these things again. This is something you can do in the next twenty-four hours.

Talk about peaceful means of dealing with problems, not allowing even your words to promote injury and harm. Let your words bring peace into others' lives and hearts. Work on your own consciousness. Purify yourself so that you are free from anger, free from hatred, free from wanting anyone to suffer either at your own hand or in any other manner.

Don't buy endangered plants, animals, or products from exploited species (furs, ivory, reptile skin and tortoise shell).

Volunteer your time to help groups who are sincerely working for a peaceful world. Learn more about other cultures and philosophies, so your appreciation of them is genuine and deep. Work to strengthen your community and the people near you. Reduce stress in your life. Be joyful. Do this and you will do much to bring peace to your part of the world. That's what Mahatma Gandhi did, and look what a difference he made. One man who lives peace truly can be an instrument of peace for many.

Querist: What are the scriptural roots of nonviolence in Hinduism?
Gurudeva: The roots of nonviolence are found in the Vedas, Upanishads, Agamas, Tirumurai, Dharma Shastras, Yoga Sutras and many other scriptures and epics. Here are a few verses from the ancient tradition of Sanatana Dharma and from our gurus and swamis:

> Let your aim be one and single. Let your hearts be joined in one--The mind at rest in unison--At peace with all, so may you be. *Rig Veda* : X.191.4.

> Peace be the earth, peaceful the ether, peaceful heaven, peaceful the waters, peaceful the herbs, peaceful the trees. May all gods bring me peace. May there be peace through these invocations of peace. With these invocations of peace which appease everything, I render peaceful whatever here is terrible, whatever here is cruel, whatever here is sinful. Let it become auspicious, let everything be beneficial to us. *Atharva Veda* : X.191.4.

> Nonviolence, truthfulness, nonstealing, purity, sense control: this, in brief, says Manu, is the dharma of all the four castes. *Dharma Shastras* : X.

> The twice-born should endure high-handed criticism; he should insult none. While yet in his body, he should not pick enmity with anyone; he should not return anger with anger; decried, he should say a good word. *Dharma Shastras* : VI.

The Lord said, 'Fearlessness, purity of heart, steadfastness in knowledge and devotion, almsgiving, self-control and sacrifice, study of the scriptures, austerity and uprightness, nonviolence, truth, freedom from anger, renunciation, tranquility, aversion to slander, compassion to all living beings, freedom from covetousness, gentleness, modesty, courage, patience, fortitude, purity and freedom from malice and overweening conceit--these belong to him who is born to the heritage of the gods, O Arjuna.' *Bhagavad Gita:* Chapter 16.

It is the principle of the pure in heart never to injure others, even when they themselves have been hatefully injured. *Tiru Kural* : Verse 312.

If a man inflicts sorrow on another in the morning, sorrow will come to him unbidden in the afternoon. *Tiru Kural* : Verse 319.

What is virtuous conduct? It is never destroying life, for killing leads to every other sin. *Tiru Kural* : Verse 321.

Many are the lovely flowers of worship offered to the Guru, but none lovelier than non-killing. Respect for life is the highest worship, the bright lamp, the sweet garland and unwavering devotion. *Tirumantiram* : Verse 197.

May all beings look at me with a friendly eye. May I do likewise, and may we all look on each other with the eyes of a friend. *Yajur Veda* : 36.18.

One should never do that to another which one regards as injurious to one's own self. This, in brief, is the rule of dharma. Yielding to desire and acting differently, one becomes guilty of adharma. *Mahabharata* : XVIII.113.8.

Those high-souled persons who desire beauty, faultlessness of limbs, long life, understanding, mental and physical strength and memory should abstain from acts of injury. *Mahabharata* : XVIII.115.8.

Ahimsa is the highest dharma. Ahimsa is the best tapas.
Ahimsa is the greatest gift. Ahimsa is the highest self-control.
Ahimsa is the highest sacrifice. Ahimsa is the highest power.
Ahimsa is the highest friend. Ahimsa is the highest truth.
Ahimsa is the highest teaching.
Mahabharata : XVIII.116.37-41.

Strictly speaking, no activity and no industry is possible
without a certain amount of violence, no matter how little.
Even the very process of living is impossible without a certain
amount of violence. What we have to do is to minimize it to
the greatest extent possible. Indeed, the very word
nonviolence, a negative word, means that it is an effort to
abandon the violence that is inevitable in life. Therefore,
whoever believes in *ahimsa* will engage himself in
occupations that involve the least possible violence. Mahatma
Gandhi, *My Socialism,* 34-45.

The obstacles to *yoga*--such as acts of violence and untruth--
may be directly created or indirectly caused or approved, they
may be motivated by greed, anger or self-interest, they may be
small or moderate or great, but they never cease to result in
pain and ignorance. One should overcome distracting
thoughts by remembering this. *Yoga Sutras* : II. 37.

The test of *ahimsa* is the absence of jealousy. The man whose
heart never cherishes even the thought of injury to anyone,
who rejoices at the prosperity of even his greatest enemy, that
man is the *bhakta*, he is the yogi, he is the guru of all.
Swami Vivekananda.

If you plant eggplant, you can pluck eggplants. If you sow
goodness, you can reap goodness. If you sow evil, you will
reap evil. Siva Yogaswami.

We are all of the same race and religion. We are holy beings
established in Divinity itself. This truth can be understood
only by those who have grasped it through the magical charm
of a life of *dharma*--not by other means. Because of that,

sages have emphatically proclaimed again and again that it is necessary to love all existing lives as one's own.
Siva Yogaswami.

Do good to all. God is there, within you. Don't kill. Don't harbor anger. Siva Yogaswami.

By *ahimsa* Patanjali meant the removal of the desire to kill. All forms of life have an equal right to the air of *maya*. The saint who uncovers the secret of creation will be in harmony with Nature's countless bewildering expressions. All men may understand this truth by overcoming the passion for destruction. Sri Yukteswar to Paramahansa Yogananda.

The Hindu sage who sees the whole of life . . . . If he does not fight, it is not because he rejects all fighting as futile, but because he has finished his fights. He has overcome all dissensions between himself and the world and is now at rest. . . . We shall have wars and soldiers so long as the brute in us is untamed. Dr. S. Radhakrishnan.

You do not like to suffer yourself. How can you inflict suffering on others? Every killing is a suicide. The eternal, blissful and natural state has been smothered by this life of ignorance. In this way the present life is due to the killing of the eternal, pristine Being. Is it not a case of suicide? Ramana Maharishi, June 1935.

Someone who believes in violence and continues causing injury to others can never be peaceful himself.
Swami Satchidananda.

To be free from violence is the duty of every man. No thought of revenge, hatred or ill will should arise in our minds. Injuring others gives rise to hatred.
Swami Sivananda.

O lover of meditation, become pure and clean. Observe nonviolence in mind, speech and body. Never break another's heart. Avoid wounding another's feelings. Harm no one. Help all. Neither be afraid nor frighten others.
Swami Muktananda.

May all be happy. May we never see a tear in another's eyes!
Sri Sri Sri Balagangadharnath Swamiji.

Using words that do not offend and not speaking ill of others
is *tapas* of speech. B.K.S. Iyengar.

Islamic *Wasim Siddiqui*

Since recorded history, the human race has yearned for world peace. The major religious faiths have urged their followers to strive toward the attainment of this goal. Yet, even in our present day civilization, might is still right, and the poor and weak are still brutally ruled and suppressed. The pursuits of wealth, power and fame have been the dominant endeavors of the human race. Submission to God, awareness of spiritual principles, and promotion of higher ethical values have been continuously supplanted within the individual and society by greed, self-promotion, lust, false pride, and power—each of which have been proven to be counter-productive to the pursuit of peace. Why has the human race failed to achieve universal peace? We have built lofty institutions, churches, synagogues, temples and mosques. Yet we have remained distant from the spirit and teachings of God. From Adam to Muhammad, prophets of all races and traditions have taught that worldly pursuits need not be the goal of humans, that God is the source of fulfillment of our every need. Yet the human race has demonstrated a collective ignorance of this promise of God. The simple truths that have been revealed to the human race again and again by the prophets of God all point to the fact that God exists as a Creator, as an essential part of every human being, and as the infinite provider of all our material and spiritual needs. God is the origin and exemplar of peace within each major religion.

For a Muslim, Islam, Christianity, and Judaism are but three forms of one religion. In its original purity, this was the religion and faith of Abraham, Al-Islam, which means the absolute self-surrender to the Will of God. [All references to the Qur'an are from Abdullah Yusuf Ali, Ba Holy Qur'an, U.S. ed. (New York: Tahrike Tarsile Qur'an, 1987).]

> The same religion has He established for you as that which He enjoined on Noah, which We have sent by inspiration to thee.

And that which We enjoined on Abraham, Moses and Jesus
namely, that ye should remain steadfast in religion and make
no divisions therein. (*Qur'an* XLII.13)[1].

Say ye, We believe in God and the revelation given to us,
and to Abraham, Ismail, Issac, Jacob and the Tribes, and that
given to Moses and Jesus and that given to (all) Prophets from
their Lord: We make no difference between one and another
of them; and we bow to God. (*Qur'an* II.136).

O ye Apostles! Enjoy (all) things good and pure, and work
righteousness; for I am well acquainted with (all) that ye do.
And verily this brotherhood is one and I am your lord and
Cherisher; therefore fear Me (and no other).
(*Qur'an* XXIII.51, 52).

One of the distinguishing features of Islam is the relationship
between humans and their Creator which is free from any
intermediaries. Each human being has the ability and responsibility
to communicate directly with God through their own individual
consciousness.

When my servant ask thee concerning Me, I am indeed close
(to them), I listen to the prayer of every supplicant when he
calleth on Me: let them also, with a will, listen to My call and
believe in Me that they walk in the right way. (*Qur'an*
II.186).

There is not a secret consultation between three, but He makes
thee fourth among them, nor between five but He makes the
sixth, nor between fewer nor more, but He is in their midst,
wheresoever they be. (*Qur'an* L. VIII.7).

And your Lord says, "Call on Me, I will answer your prayer!"
(*Qur'an* IL.60).

For my Lord is (always) near, ready to answer.
(*Qur'an* XI.61).

For God is nearer to him than (his) jugular vein.
(*Qur'an* L.16).

The Islamic concept of peace is derived from the unity of all existence: inanimate, plant, and animal. All activities of the cosmos are encompassed within the inner workings of the human mind. There is a unity of all energy whether it is the physical striving for necessities or the spiritual craving for elation. Islam believes that there is one faith for humankind and that this faith entails complete surrender to the Creator in both secular and spiritual matters. This idea is inherent in our mental and emotional processes. In the Islamic faith, peace is the foundation for the principle of harmony--harmony in the universe, in the natural laws of life and in the origin of human beings. Islam also maintains that God is an essential part of every person's consciousness. As such, God is ever aware of each individual's prayers and needs. By learning to follow the Will of God as it is revealed within individual consciousness, every human being may discover their material and spiritual needs abundantly filled with peace as the reward. Islam believes that it is imperative that the individual human being be at peace with himself or herself before the goal of universal peace may be realized. Therefore, Islam, through its teachings in the *Qur'an* and *Hadith,* aims to implant peace within the individual's innermost conscience.

By focusing upon the individual first, Islam acknowledges the uniqueness of each person's instincts and ambitions as being individual expressions and creations of God. The term *jihad* literally means effort or endeavor. In religious connotation, it applies to the whole effort of the individual Muslim to realize the sovereignty of God within their inner conscience. "The greatest *Jihad* is that against a man's own lust" (*Hadith: Sayings of Prophet Mohammed).* This *jihad* takes place within the individual's own heart and mind until an awareness develops that there truly exists only one Will within individual conscience, and that is the sweet and pleasurable Will of God. The term *jihad* is also applicable to patience under persecution, to active charity, and indeed to every form of human endeavor which aims at self-improvement and greater awareness of God. For instance, the term "*Al-Jihad ul-Akbar*" (the greatest *jihad)* is applied by Prophet Muhammad, to the effort of the student to become learned and the effort of the learned to spread knowledge. "The ink of the scholar is more holy than the blood of the martyr" (*Hadith: Sayings of Prophet Mohammad).*

Thus, in Islam, the needs, interests, ideals, and goals of society and humanity at large are realized first at the individual level.

In striving to inculcate such a living relationship with God, the teachings of Islam transform individual character. The transformed person, although outwardly associating with people, places and things, is nevertheless inwardly with God. In the midst of a crowd, the transformed person dwells in the spiritual retreat of the Divine Secret. This person, though perhaps running here and there in pursuit of material goals and experiencing events both bitter and sweet, pleasant and unpleasant, beautiful and ugly, has yet a heart that is free. Such an individual exists in a world of tranquility in which the Face of God is seen everywhere he or she looks. The teachings of Islam strive to inculcate a positive peace that will exalt and enrich life. Every aspect of life, from birth to marriage to death is meant to be experienced to build character and strengthen faith in God and love for humanity. Everything and everyone that one touches or sees is to be treated with reverence as a beloved creation of God. Hence, conscientious Muslims, those dedicated to unveiling the Will of God for their personal lives, extend their spiritual life into every aspect of their material life. So, irrespective of wherever they are or whatever they are doing, such people are always close to God.

A true Muslim seeks to follow the Will of God as it is revealed within individual consciousness. Through obedience to the Will of God, prayer and meditation, individuals realize their closeness to God and become aware of God's mercy and compassion. Obedience to the "inner-voice," prayer and meditation become a way of life as the individual experiences more and more of the love and Grace of God in his or her life. The knowledge that their individual consciousness will reveal the Will of God for their lives gives great inner strength to individuals to pursue righteous paths without fear of obstacles such as conflict with people who claim to have personal power, wealth and influence that is not God-given. With a living faith that Allah (God) is always in one's thoughts (consciousness) and actions, and that Allah is able to guide and provide abundance, the individual attains inner peace and contributes to the external peace of societies.

Islam emphasizes the character of the individual. Individuals are the nucleus of society. They embody the Spirit of God which is incorporated into their own consciousness. When they are attentive to this consciousness, the Spirit of God is manifested through their conduct. Islam sees the individual as the nucleus of the family and the family as the nucleus of society. Through its teachings, Islam strives to transform the individual into a peace-loving person both in thought and action. Islam believes that peace in the individual's inner mind creates peace at home which leads to peace within the society. To encourage this, besides broader spiritual guidance, Islam has outlined specific codes of conduct and laws for individual members of the family. The rights and duties of spouses, children, parents, and extended family members are all considered. For instance, the Islamic code of life strongly prohibits the use of alcohol, drugs, and sensual allurements. These acts are considered to have serious adverse effects on the peace and harmony of the family. When one has a realization of personal peace and an awareness of a personal relationship with God, then one will act in accordance with one's God-given purpose and there would be no need to compete for a limited resource since God would provide for each person uniquely according to the Will which was given them to fulfill. Such a society would be based upon peace, since each individual would be revealing and contributing to the wholeness of God.

In conclusion, Islam promotes peace in society by emphasizing to individuals their role as the recipients of God's grace and the custodians of the earth. Islam reminds us that we were all individual expressions of God created from one Soul. The spiritual principle of equality that makes no distinction between black and white, man and woman, noble and humble, rich and poor, strong and weak, educated and uneducated, is strictly emphasized. Islam strongly encourages compassion, tolerance and love toward all human beings. In Islam, the path to be followed in life has been designed in such a way that man's social and material life is like a cradle in which the spiritual life is nurtured. The balance of the individual's human experience and spiritual development fosters the growth of God-awareness and initiates an inner peace which is active, not passive. God-awareness grows into an obedience to the Will of God which, in turn, fosters the creation of inner peace. This peace grows as the individual recognizes the oneness and omnipotence of God and realizes that God's justice is the basis for achieving social equilibrium and cooperation. Thus, in Islam, world peace may be attained through the evolution of the passions and desires of individual consciousness into an inner harmony of obedience to God's Will. This creates an awareness that the family is the support and expression of each individual member's God-spirit which leads to the creation of a vital, harmonious peace among societies and nations.

SUGGESTED READING

AUTHOR'S NOTE: The author gratefully acknowledges the invaluable contributions of Susan M. Lofton to the writing and editing of this paper and would like to suggest the following books for the interested reader of Islam:

Khan, Fateh Ullah. *God, Universe and Man, The Holy Qur'an and the Hereafter*. Lahore, Pakistan: Wajidalis, 1982.

Kotb, Sayed. *Social Justice in Islam*. New York: Octagon Books, 1970.

Qutb, Syed. *In the Shade of Al-Qur'an*. Bangladesh: Islamic Cultural Center, 1981.

Rahman, Fazlur. *Islam*. Chicago: University of Chicago Press, 1979.

Jewish *Ira J. Lichton*

This Jewish view of peace is being expressed during the week when Jews all over the world are celebrating Pesach (Passover), an auspicious time in the Jewish year, a time which coincides with the Christian Holy Week (Easter Week). Since Jewish tradition does not require a fixed set of beliefs for all, what follows represents only what I personally know of Jewish tradition. The word for peace in the Hebrew language is well known—it is *shalom*. This word, usually translated as "peace", actually means more than this—it signifies welfare of every kind: security, contentment, sound health, prosperity, friendship, peace of mind and heart, as opposed to the dissatisfaction and unrest caused by evil (Isaiah:17; 48:22). Etymologically, it denotes completeness in the sense of wholeness and therefore lack of any violent harm to the body. This fits with the idea that peace is not just the absence of war, but rather includes good relations between people and nations and, perhaps most important, absence of any cause for war. Mere absence of war is perhaps truce, but not real peace.

In the Jewish tradition faith, while important, does not carry as much weight as deeds do. Deeds, in turn, are guided by law, and the Jewish view of law is laid down in many written documents beginning with the Torah, the earliest part of the Bible. Jewish law extends to post-biblical laws, embedded in the Talmud and related works of the period, and, by further extension to the civil and criminal laws of today. Willingness to amend and update Jewish law and to respect the law has served historically as a civilizing force and a safeguard against fundamentalism.

Roots of Nonviolence

Jewish law gives human beings dominion over animals (Genesis:24) [all biblical references in this chapter refer to *The Holy*

71

Scriptures According to the Masoretic Text, Philadelphia, The Jewish Publication Society of America, 1955] and thus allows killing of animals for food. This law is interpreted not to allow the killing of animals for the sake of killing per se, but rather as a means of sustaining human life. Although animals may be killed for food they may not be killed needlessly or killed in an inhumane way. This law is detailed in the Babylonian Talmud (the fifth division of the Mishnah, Sanctities, third part, Chullin) in twelve chapters on ritual slaughter. The law is expressed today in the careful way that livestock is slaughtered in most slaughterhouses. It is forbidden to slaughter a young animal in front of its mother, since this would cause mental pain. According to Maimonides (*The Guide of the Perplexed,* part 3, chapter 48), "For in these cases animals feel very great pain, there being no difference regarding this pain between man and the other animals." There is a current of Jewish thought that argues for following this portion of the law simply by consuming no animal food at all. Whether this will become part of Jewish law in the future is not yet clear. On the Sabbath, animals, like man, must be given rest (Deuteronomy:14).

The nourishing and protecting of human life is of first importance in Jewish law. This idea is first expressed in the proscription against murder (Exodus:13). Not only is life not to be taken deliberately, but saving an endangered life is a commandment of such importance that it supersedes all other laws of the Torah, provided, however, that life is not saved in exchange for the commission of murder, adultery or idolatry. This issue was illustrated for me in a forceful way in 1989 when I was on sabbatical leave with my wife in Israel. Although one must not work or drive a motor vehicle on the Sabbath or on one of the High Holidays of the Jewish Year (particularly Yom Kippur, the day of repentance), this rule does not apply when a life is in danger. Imagine my dismay and that of others upon finding that some Jewish fundamentalists stoned an ambulance carrying a patient to hospital on Yom Kippur! This was a clear violation of Jewish (and Israeli) law and illustrates the yawning gulf between Jewish law and the practice of fundamentalists.

Causes of Violence

Having been victimized by violence and war over many centuries, Jews are perhaps as sensitive as any people to the maltreatment of people wherever it occurs. A small number of Jewish civil rights workers labored alongside Dr. Martin Luther King, and some gave their lives. These workers saw the injustice of racism and all that it entails. It is in the Jewish record that prophets arose from time to time, risking the wrath of the civil authorities to demand redress of injustice. There is no doubt in my mind that Dr. King was a modern prophet, inspired by the biblical verse: "And the Lord spoke unto Moses: 'go in unto Pharaoh and say unto him: Thus Saith the Lord: Let My people go, that they may serve Me'" (Exodus:26). The importance of redressing injustice is that if it is not done, violence will follow. This leads directly to the Jewish idea that peace can have no meaning if injustice remains as a potential cause of violence and war. If you consider South Africa today you will see that this concept is not a mere abstraction but has direct practical importance.

The Passover Haggadah (book of readings) contains a number of references to causes of violence. One of these is glorification of violence in the causes of freedom. It specifically states that the liberation of the Jews from bondage in Egypt was to be considered as having been accomplished by the Deity alone, and not by force of arms exerted by the Israelites themselves:

> 'For I will go through the land of Egypt in that night' (Exodus:12) I *and not any intermediary.* Now, obviously the Holy One, blessed be He, could have given the Children of Israel the power to *avenge themselves* upon the Egyptians, but He did not want to sanction the use of their fists for self-defense even at that time; for, at that moment they might merely have defended themselves against evil-doers, by such means the way of the fist spreads throughout the world, and in the end defenders become aggressors [*A Passover Haggadah,* the New Union Haggadah, revised edition, (New York: Central Conference of American Rabbis, 1974), p. 44].

The angels themselves are chastised for condoning violence:

> Our rabbis taught: When the Egyptian armies were drowning
> in the sea, the Heavenly Hosts broke out in songs of
> jubilation. God silenced them and said, 'My creatures are
> perishing and you sing praises?' (Babylonian Talmud,
> Sanhedrin, verse 39b in *A Passover Haggadah,* p. 48).

And, finally:

> Our rabbis taught: 'The sword comes into the world because
> of justice delayed and justice denied' (Pirkei Avot, *Sayings
> of the Fathers,* chapter 5, verse 8 in *A Passover Haggadah,*
> p.49).

Is violence or killing ever justified? Jewish law, like
American civil law, allows self-defense. Both permit killing in self-
defense. However, it must be noted that killing in self-defense is
not allowed if there is any alternative. Police personnel, for
example, may not fire at unarmed persons or even at armed persons
who do not directly and immediately pose a threat to life. In war,
killing is unavoidable, and so it is in war itself which must be
avoided, if possible. This point is clear to anyone who watched the
story of the invasion of Panama in 1989 unfold.

Jewish tradition allows war in some circumstances, but never
glorifies it. On the contrary, a prayer for peace is recited weekly:
"Grant peace and happiness, blessing and mercy, to all Israel and to
all the world. Bless us, our God, all of us together, with the light of
your presence, for in the light of your presence we have found a
teaching of life, the love of mercy, the law of justice, and the way of
peace: for it is ever Your will that Your people Israel be blessed
with peace."

Causes of Nonviolence

Within the framework of Jewish practice the exceptions to
killing, noted above, are strictly limited--humane killing of animals
for food and self-defense in certain carefully laid out circumstances.
Otherwise Jewish law forbids violence, and this has been for

centuries the ideal for peoples of the Jewish-Christian tradition as well as for all civilized people of the world. The question arises as to how an ideal of nonviolence can be achieved. A Jewish view would be that there is no magic way to accomplish this. Judaism is not a religion in the secular sense of the term, but rather a guide to life, much like that put forward by Hawaiian community leaders. If violence is to end, it can only be because virtually all rational members of the community want it that way, and because there is no compelling reason to be violent. In the Jewish view, the first condition is often met. It therefore remains to work on achieving the second condition, namely, that there must be an absence of any cause to disturb the peace.

In this view, combating injustice and poverty became the primary tools for achieving nonviolence within a given community. In some instances, a motive remains--the drive to consume illegal drugs. This motive usually, but not always, arises from poverty and a disintegrated home and family life. Where it does not, it may be said that the consumer is no longer a rational member of the community. For Jews, the reason for working against injustice and poverty is not an altruistic motive of doing good for its own sake, but rather a practical matter of protection for self, family and community. The Jewish view, incidentally, does not see humans as fundamentally evil, or for that matter good. It merely recognizes that people have to live and get along with each other and has, over the years, evolved certain rules of behavior and law.

On a world scale, matters are somewhat more complex, but the principles are the same: to eliminate violence one must eliminate poverty and injustice, and also curb the ability of irrational leaders to influence policy. History abounds with examples of what happens when this is not done. Rather than dwell on such history, called by Gibbon "history; which is, indeed, little more than the register of the crimes, follies, and misfortunes of mankind" (*Decline and Fall of the Roman Empire*, chapter 3), let us consider the possibilities of peace.

Transition from Violence to Nonviolence

My trip to Israel often made me ask whether that nation will be blessed with peace. Peace has been a very scarce commodity in that part of the world. Lebanon has been in constant turmoil and civil war, and recently has seen fighting not only among Moslems and between Christians and Moslems, but now even Christian against Christian. Of all Israel's neighbors, only Egypt has signed a peace treaty with her. The others remain technically at war, but argue that Israel should give up territory without a peace treaty in order to give nationhood to the Palestinian people. Meanwhile violence abounds in the West Bank and Gaza; Arabs are being killed by other Arabs and by Israelis. Arabs kill fellow Arabs suspected of cooperating with the Israeli authorities, and Israeli soldiers kill Arabs who threaten their lives with stones.

The transition from violence to nonviolence must, as noted above, be one in which the causes of violence are removed. The case of Israel and her neighbors may serve as an example as complex as any. In my view, Israel must press on with efforts to redress differences by negotiation. This will first require a stable Israeli government which enjoys the support of a substantial majority of its people and which is committed to the peace process. Second, this will, as a counterpart, require a Palestinian delegation which has the support of its people and the latitude to negotiate. As to the first requirement, an Israeli government which had balked at accepting American terms for peace negotiations has now fallen and efforts are underway to form a new one. Israelis generally want to have peace but are hindered by several factors. Leaving aside the question of the role of legitimate Arab governments and of the PLO, there is the factor that Israel, forced into a role analogous to that of a colonizing power in 1967 [see Emmanuel Sivan, "The Intifada and Decolonization", *Middle East Review*, 22, 2 (Winter 1989/1990), pp. 2-6] has little experience that would show her how to reach an agreement with a subject people as, for example, the French did in Algeria.

The second requirement is a Palestinian delegation with credible leaders. Whether such a delegation will arise by efforts of the Palestinian Arabs themselves, or will arise out of a plan for elections in the West Bank and Gaza, as proposed by former Prime Minister Shamir, or via some other plan remains to be seen. Just as Israel must prepare for negotiations, so must Palestinian Arabs be reminded that violence will not solve their problems. The key to resolution of this or any other international crisis of peace rests in the substitution of negotiation, however difficult, for rioting, bloodshed, and war. As I write, the news is full of another (and very different) crisis involving Lithuanian secession, in which the transition from the threat of violence to a nonviolent solution must also rest upon negotiations to remove the causes of conflict. Such negotiations can succeed only if they are fair to both sides. The concept of fairness or justice for avoiding conflict is basic to Jewish tradition. The Jewish view of what people must do to fulfill the commandments of the Deity rejects ritualistic fervor in favor of instituting justice, as we may read from the writings of the prophet Amos (5:21-24):

> I hate, I despise your feasts,
> And I will take no delight in your solemn assemblies.
> Yea, though ye offer me burnt offerings and your meal-
> offerings,
> I will not accept them;
> Neither will I regard the peace-offerings of your fat beasts.
> Take thou away from Me the noise of thy songs;
> And let Me not hear the melody of thy psalteries.
> But let justice well up as waters,
> And righteousness as a mighty stream.

Characteristics of a Nonviolent Society

Descriptions of Utopias abound in literature; Jews today do not look to find a perfect (and therefore completely nonviolent) society. In previous times, the concept arose that such a society would be instituted when the Messiah would come. Until then, the idea was to pray for and to await the coming of the Messiah. Modern Jews have modified this concept; they speak of a messianic age, namely an age during which people take responsibility for creating a perfect society and work for it. The Messiah is a process, not a person. And the process is not something to be awaited but rather something to be engaged in, something to do in order to help create a better, if not perfect world. The messianic age would be an age of universal peace and prosperity, and of course an age in which there would be a totally nonviolent society. Jewish literature has many references to such an age, for example the description by Isaiah (65:21-25):

> And they shall build houses, and inhabit them;
> And they shall plant vineyards, and eat the fruit of them.
> They shall not build and another inhabit,
> They shall not plant, and another eat;
> For as the days of a tree shall be the days of My people,
> And Mine elect shall long enjoy the work of their hands.
> They shall not labor in vain, Nor bring forth for terror;
> For they are the seed blessed of the Lord,
> And their offspring with them.
> And it shall come to pass that, before they call I will answer,
> And while they are yet speaking, I will hear.
> The wolf and the lamb shall feed together,
> And the lion shall eat straw like the ox;
> And dust shall be the serpent's food.
> They shall not hurt nor destroy
> In all My holy mountain, saith the Lord.

And, centuries later, Maimonides wrote, "In the messianic days there will be no hunger or war, no jealousy or strife; prosperity will be universal and the world's predominant occupation will be to know the Lord" (Yad, Melakhim 12:2,5). The themes persist that the messianic age must be devoid not only of violence but also of hunger and injustice which provokes violence.

Recently an advertisement was circulated for the periodical *Peace & Change,* published by Sage Periodicals Press in association with the Council on Peace Research in History and the Consortium on Peace Research, Education and Development. On the front page of the notice there is a quotation by Anatol Rappaport of the University of Toronto: "*Peace & Change* is particularly valuable to peace researchers and peace educators. . . . It puts peace activities in historical perspective and it emphasizes the fundamental structural connection between peace and social justice." Embedded in this quotation is the idea of the fundamental connection between peace and social justice so often pointed out by Jewish writers.

What Should be Done to Move Society Toward Less Violence?

It is the job of many leaders and skilled thinkers to answer such a large question. A Jewish view would be that a messianic age must have not only peace but also the conditions that let peace be achieved, namely justice and prosperity. Thus to move society toward more nonviolent conditions is to move society toward more social justice and better living conditions. This is no small task, and writing about it does not accomplish it; however one value of this formulation is that it points out the correct directions in which to move. There is a further condition: one must also speak and teach continually for nonviolence, pointing out that to achieve it one must work to eliminate the conditions that breed violence. This is the work of the Institute for Peace, of every thinking person.

Dr. Martin Luther King, Jr., who spoke for peace with the voice of a modern prophet, was well aware of the fact that to move toward peace it would be necessary to move also toward justice and prosperity. In his last book he wrote [*Where Do We Go from Here: Chaos or Community,* (New York: Bantam Books, 1967), p. 157]:

> All these questions remind us that there is a need for a radical restructuring of the architecture of American society. For its very survival's sake, America must re-examine old presuppositions and release itself from many things that for centuries have been held sacred. For the evils of racism, poverty and militarism to die, a new set of values must be born. . . . Let us therefore not think of our movement as one that seeks to integrate the Negro into all the existing values of American society. Let us be those creative dissenters who will call our beloved nation to a higher destiny, to a new plateau of compassion, to a more noble expression of humaneness.

These words, as much as any uttered in Dr. King's well-known speeches, carry the essence of prophecy.

Today, more than ever the issue of peace remains paramount. One can work for peace and one can hope with the prophet Isaiah (2:4):

And He shall judge between the nations,
And shall decide for many peoples;
And they shall beat their swords into plowshares,
And their spears into pruning-hooks;
Nation shall not lift up sword against nation,
Neither shall they learn war any more.

SUGGESTED READINGS

Ausubel, Nathan. *The Book of Jewish Knowledge*. New York: Crown, 1964. ("Peace, Jewish Concept of"), p. 329.

Birnbaum, Philip. *Encyclopedia of Jewish Concepts*. Brooklyn: Hebrew Publishing, 1979.

Branch, Taylor. *Parting the Waters: America in the King Years 1954-63*. New York: Simon and Schuster, 1988.

Dawidowicz, Lucy S. *The War Against the Jews 1933-1945*. New York: Bantam, 1976.

Eban, Abba. *Heritage: Civilization and the Jews*. New York: Summit, 1984.

Herzog, Chaim. *The Arab-Israeli Wars: War and Peace in the Middle East from the War of Independence through Lebanon*. New York: Vintage, 1984.

Kerzer, Morris N. *What is a Jew?* 4th ed. New York: Collier, 1978.

King, Martin Luther, Jr. *Where Do We Go From Here: Chaos or Community?* New York: Bantam, 1968.

Schiff, Ze'ev and Ya'ari Ehud. *Israel's Lebanon War*. London: George Allen & Unwin, 1984.

Steinsaltz, Adin. *The Essential Talmud*. London: Weidenfeld and Nicholson, 1976.

Religious Society of Friends (Quaker)

Ruth Anna Brown

One of the better-known pacifist Christian faiths is the Religious Society of Friends, commonly known as "Quakers" or "Friends." Established by George Fox in England in 1649, its peaceful ideas stemmed from the concept that there was a "Universal Plan" for all of humanity which included a "God"--a "purpose" so to speak--which was larger than themselves and beyond human authority.

Quakers believe that there is a spark of that Divine purpose present in each person. This makes it possible to look to the Spirit of God for final authority, while at the same time expecting all persons to use their own Divine Spark for the good of humankind.

Because that Divine Spirit is larger than our human selves, and yet is found within us, we are also sacred. We have a "Light Within." In the early writings of Friends there were constant references to that Inner Light, the Inward Light, the Seed, the Christ Within, the Eternal Christ, the Divine Principle, or "that of God in every person."

Faith and Practice, the Quakers' "Book of Christian Discipline," explains how this concept became a part of their truth. It refers to the lack of ritual or clergy involved in the Services, and to the fact that Christ speaks directly to each human soul. Because each human is endowed with a measure of the Divine Spirit, then Love, the outworking of the Divine Spirit, becomes the most potent influence which can be applied to the affairs of humans.

Since the time of its inception--more than three hundred years ago--the Society of Friends has worked for a genuine and lasting peace: peace between individuals, peace and justice within societies and peace and justice among nations of the world. It is that "peace testimony" which makes the Society of Friends so well known; that "justice" which seeks to include racial and social issues while harboring the spirit of good will to all persons. We must, insist the Quakers, have the willingness to see good in those who differ from us and we must be willing to have a working spirit of reconciliation.

This spark of the Divine which they believed to be within every person also led the Quakers to the teaching of equality between men and women. This was a new philosophy not usually observed in religious communities! Because of that philosophy, many Quaker women overcame their fear of public testimony and became strong advocates for peace and justice. Some women, such as Elizabeth Fry, worked for prison reform; others tackled slavery and the rights of women. We of this century point with great pride to such leading Quaker women as Margaret Fell, Lucretia Mott, Susan B. Anthony, and the sisters Angelina and Sarah Grimke.

The Light which leads to unity in the Quaker Meeting illuminates all their relations between people. That Light has led the Friends into deep concern for Indians, Negroes, and other minority groups who have been victims of prejudice or exploitation. It has inspired the work done for prisoners and the mentally ill. It has created a testimony for the peaceful ways of resolving human conflicts. It has aroused a growing concern for a social order in which the fullest opportunity can be given for the expression and development of that Divine potentiality with which all human beings are endowed.

Quakers who thoughtfully and spiritually have considered the causes of war have come to the conclusion that war has never been in accordance with the will of God. They therefore try to act as peacemakers in all human relationships, in all private and business affairs, and in all national and international dealings. Because they believe that if changes of government are needed those changes can be made without violence, they are opposed to the training of youth for war and they regard military conscription as an offense to the human spirit and as inconsistent with the teaching and practice of Christianity.

Believing that the Divine Light Within is also the Holy Spirit and that the two cannot be separated, the Quakers refuse all acts of violence. If that refusal springs from a sincere and deep reverence and love for "that of God" in an opponent's nature, then it will be potent enough to reach out and win that person's soul. In other words, the "power of vibrations" is translated into the"power of love."

These truths became the basis of a document which the Quakers presented to King Charles II in 1600. The writer was Margaret Fell, the woman who was destined to become the wife of George Fox. Some have called her the co-founder of the Society of Friends because of her many years of self-sacrificing work on behalf of the Quakers; others have referred to her as the Mother of Quakerism.

Based on that declaration, the Philadelphia Yearly Meetings of the Religious Society of Friends adopted the following statement in 1938:

> We declare our faith in those abiding truths taught and exemplified by Jesus Christ--that every individual of every race and nation, is of supreme worth; that love is the highest law of life, and that evil is to be overcome, not by further evil, but by good. The relationship of nation to nation, of race to race, of class to class must be based on this Divine law of love, if peace and progress are to be achieved. We believe in those principles, not as mere ideals for some future time, but as part of the eternal moral order and as a way of life to be lived here and now. War is a colossal violation of this way of life. If we are true to our faith we can have no part in it.
>
> We affirm the supremacy of conscience. We recognize the privileges and obligations of citizenship; but we reject as false that philosophy which sets the state above moral law and demands from the individual unquestioning obedience to every state command. On the contrary, we assert that every individual, while owing loyalty to the state, owes a more binding loyalty to a higher authority--the authority of God and conscience (*Faith and Practice*, 1955).

Those thoughts were eventually to become a part of the "Queries." Queries, or questions, enable individuals to examine themselves in relation to their Christian standards. Query No. 12 asks a question concerning "Human Brotherhood":

1. Do you live in the life and power which takes away the occasion of all wars?
2. Do you seek to take your part in the ministry of reconciliation between individuals, groups, and nations?
3. Do you faithfully maintain our testimony against military training and other preparation for war and against participation in war as inconsistent with the spirit and teaching of Christ?

These questions of "do you?" became questions of "how can we?" How can we seek to take part in the ministry of reconciliation between individuals, groups, and nations? It was obvious that all Quakers wanted to be a part of that ministry of reconciliation, but not all Quakers had the ability, the time, nor the means to work actively against war. True enough, but they could make sure that they worked in the spirit of reconciliation as individuals, as partners, and as families. But it was not always easy to find time to work against war when the work of keeping body and soul together had to be the first consideration.

With this in mind, the organization called the American Friends Service Committee (AFSC) was started in 1917. The AFSC became the "action arm" of the Society of Friends. As the organization grew it included not only Quakers but other persons and organizations dedicated to peaceful means of solving disputes. The Committee's brief treatise, *Quaker Approaches to Human Brotherhood*, reads in part:

> The transforming power of spiritual life is no less a force today than it was in the days of George Fox, seventeenth century Quaker leader. Friends today believe that the authority and power for all action must stem from an inner seeking, and that all may share, as seekers, in the revelation of God's will. This spiritual democracy points the way to a world wherein all men and women may realize their "fit place and service."
>
> That this Divine Power may be realized by all people, and that the true brotherhood of man may come about as the natural outcome of this realization, is the concern of the Society of Friends. In the American Friends Service Committee workers and seekers from all groups, in natural

harmonious association, try to develop a climate wherein this deeper brotherhood may thrive. In its projects, men and women are encouraged to find for themselves a way of life that will lead to a growing realization of this power.

The belief in "that of God in every man" brings about the respect for, and faith in, every individual so necessary today to offset the disregard for human rights which is the natural outcome and result of war. Prejudice and hatred are burdens heavy on the shoulders of those who carry them and upon those against whom they are directed. It is to free people from these burdens that the work of the Committee in the field of race relations is directed. The time is short. The task is great, and at best the work of the American Friends Service Committee can be but a leavening of the whole. (*Faith and Practice*, p. 216).

During those first years the American Friends Service Committee focused on relief work. During and after World War I they provided help in rebuilding the war-torn cities by giving relief and medical assistance in France, Vienna, Serbia, Poland, Russia, Turkey, and Greece.

They provided assistance to the refugees in the 1930s and 1940s from Spain, Germany, Poland, Holland, Belgium, and parts of Asia. They proudly accepted the Nobel Peace Prize for their relief work in 1947.

But the Quakers were interested in stopping wars before they began. Their concept of the "Light Within" every person could not accept war with its cruelty, its disregard for human rights, and its economic devastation. First they considered the causes of war which were clearly visible: poverty, unemployment, inflation, sadism and masochism, anger and hatred. Greed, too, was, and is, certainly one of the main causes of war, whether personal greed or governmental and national greed. Some governments are able to overcome the people's abhorrence of war by referring to the conflict as a "just war." But Quakers have long objected to definitions such as "just wars," saying any kind of war, however small and for whatever reason, is wrong. Compliance with wrong is dangerous in *all* cases.

As they continued to question, they began to ask themselves whether one could object to a war being waged by one's government and still make use of that government's services. Because the government's service is so all-inclusive, because the entire economic system is based on its rules and regulations, it is difficult to segregate the amount of taxes one feels one should withhold as a protest against war usage. Would it even be possible, they questioned, to withhold a small amount to salve one's conscience--or must one withdraw from society altogether?

The choice was a bitter one and Quakers could not agree. But they could agree on the need for a kinship of humans, the need to develop a sense of human solidarity with the peoples of the world.

To that end they began the use of Quaker "Centers" where people of different habits, opinions, languages, and religions might have the opportunity to meet in a friendly atmosphere. Mediation and love, they hoped, could be used by people working in small groups and the idea of nonviolence might lead to the creation of a new and better society. The people might, perhaps, adopt the idea that war is not inherent, essential, or even an inevitable element in our world!

In 1965 the American Friends Service Committee was asked to prepare a report on "The Nonviolent Defense of a Nation." That report was incorporated into the book entitled *In Place of War* which identifies three different purposes for the use of nonviolent actions:

1. Nonviolent action which can be used as a means of social protest, social reform, and social revolution. The nonviolent movement would consist of the means of creating a just and stable society--within the bounds of the government already formed.

2. Nonviolent action which could be used as a means of maintaining social order during social protest. In this case, one would try to preserve the present social order, and this pertains mainly to the use of the government (the police) controlling by nonviolent means. Nonviolent techniques can also be used in the care of the mentally ill and toward those confined in prisons.

3. Nonviolent action as a means of national defense. Quoting directly, "It is conceivable, of course, that in the event of war or threat of war, a nonviolent anti-war campaign could be mounted in protest against the military policies of the government and could win

such wide support that the government would either go out of power or else adopt a policy of nonmilitary defense."

Nonviolence, then, can be used against one's own nation if it is not adhering to the social norms which the culture wishes to follow. That nonviolence can take many forms--it can use the power of the ordinary citizens such as the worker, the business person, the lawyer, the scholar, the editor, and the entertainer. The coffee houses of Eastern European countries have long been the habitat of dissident entertainers who spread, via music and song, their dissatisfaction with the regimes. Usually called "folk" music, the songs are either revolutionary songs or nostalgic peace songs which tell of a hope for a better world. Folk singers in the United States also have used music to encourage their followers as well as to spread their stories of dissatisfaction. A particularly well-known and loved song is the one used by the Civil Rights movement and associated with Martin Luther King, Jr., "We Shall Overcome."

It is interesting to note that dissidents and folk singers have used this song at many meetings from Siberia to Africa, from the East to the West, and one often catches snatches of its melancholy, yet hopeful, melody in the midst of pockets of humanity striving for justice worldwide.

Richard B. Gregg, in his book, *The Power of Nonviolence* (1966), gives ten historical illustrations of nonviolent action which succeeded in defying government terror, but often not without the added encouragement from individuals such as Ferenc Deak, a Catholic landowner of Hungary who protested the people's weakness and refusal to resist. "Your laws," he said, "are violated, yet your mouths remain closed! Woe to the nation that raises no protest when its rights are outraged! It contributes to its own slavery by its silence. The nation that submits to injustice and oppression without protest is doomed."

Ferenc Deak went ahead to map out a plan of nonviolent action, and with his encouragement the populace won their battle.

Hungary, South Africa, India, Norway, and Denmark are a few of the countries listed by Gregg as examples of popular resistance to their government. Many groups and individuals--not only Quakers--use nonviolent resistance, of course. Gregg names such internationally known figures as Lao-Tzu, Buddha, the

Tirtankaras, Jesus, St. Francis of Assisi, Henry David Thoreau, and Leo Tolstoy.

The United States has itself had some experience in the use of nonviolent action as a means of protest. This method was used by the citizens who were objecting to the Vietnam war. As the war became increasingly unpopular with the citizens, the American government withdrew from Vietnam. The reluctance of the citizens to wage this war, the dissatisfaction of the military with the way the war was conducted, and the continued protest by the peace action groups, as well as the protests conducted by ordinary citizens, showed the government a great underlying truth: wars cannot be waged, nor won, unless the people give their support.

Equally true is the concept that government power is "fragile" and that it would be difficult for a government to govern without a populace which agreed with its policies. "Its authority," to quote from AFSC, "rests upon the willingness of the people to obey."

In the light of today's remarkable examples of the power of nonviolence it is appropriate to consider the nations of Eastern Europe who have now succeeded in overthrowing governments which were unresponsive to public demands. Each country attacked its problem in its own way. Poland, for example, worked through its labor unions. At least one of the dissident countries has elected a parallel government in the hope of overthrowing the disliked regime.

Although we know that many Quakers stayed in the Eastern European confines after the separation of the East and West countries by the Potsdam Conference, it is sometimes difficult to ascertain the amount of influence they and their political arm, the American Friends Service Committee, were able to exercise. It was true that because of their faith and their practice of nonviolence they were able to keep alive their spirit of love and to reject the violence of the postwar years. For example, in East Germany the sons of the members of the Society of Friends were allowed conscientious objector status, and Friends were allowed to continue their Sunday meetings without incident.

Knowing the degree of passion with which Quakers surround their faith, it is not difficult to believe that they, among other Christians, fanned the flame of resistance.

In November of 1989 when the people of East Germany took their first purposeful strides through the streets of Berlin and

Leipzig, it did not resemble a well-planned peace action. Spontaneous as it seemed in the beginning, the protests gathered strength and speed so rapidly that they practically "blew open the wall!" It was the homemade signs which arose in the crowd that led one to believe long-time planning had been in process.

"NO VIOLENCE," shouted the signs; "no violence," whispered the protestors. Later in the early evening as the darkness descended upon the cities, candles appeared in the hands of the dissenters. The lights wound their way deeper and deeper into the city until the very quietness of the marchers and the lights of the candles produced an aura of mysticism.

Earlier the day before and late into the evening the churches had been filled with the leaders of the peace movement. During those meetings, too, there had been quiet and intense instructions: "No violence, remember, no violence."

The government of the German Democratic Republic collapsed; within days the "wall" started to disintegrate, but not before the young and old climbed on top of the wall and sang their songs of victory.

Romania was another of the countries in which the government was overthrown by the people. But Romania was a different story--not one of love and peace and nonviolent resistance, but one filled with hate and anger.

However, we cannot make the assumption that Romania's lack of discipline might prove our plan of nonviolent resistance ineffective. Although it might indeed prove that nonviolent resistance cannot succeed in a violent society. It might prove that unless the people are ready to accept the plan of action presented by their leaders, that plan will prove ineffective. One might also consider whether the government itself might need to be amenable to the change of politics, and, therefore, supportive to the peace movement.

We have mentioned in this essay war and the causes of war; we have considered the need for nonviolence in the world. It is obvious that individuals and groups will need to change from the concept of international violence to that of international nonviolence. There is at present not only the possibility of an accidental nuclear war, but the likelihood of terrorist attacks. War can no longer be regarded as "rational"--if, indeed, it ever could have been so regarded.

Perhaps we should look at "why war?" again. Why do we have wars? Overall we must take into account the seemingly universal desire for more than one needs, that desire called "greed." Certainly individuals have that desire, some more than others, but nations are greedy too. They have the "need" to annex other territories, the "need" to have more and better nuclear bombs, newer and bigger nuclear ships, larger and more expensive bombers. When nations have those methods of destroying their neighbors, they will also have the "need" to use them--to "try them out" so to speak.

If we add to the above the poverty of the citizens whose means of survival has been usurped, and if they have been taught to hate by their governments--then the fuse has been lit.

The members of the committee who prepared the pamphlet, *In Place of War*, commented that the purpose of civilian defense is to defend. They suggested three tests which a civilian defense initiative would need to possess: (1) it would need to provide a means of defense in case of attack, (2) it would need to contribute to the development of a foreign policy acceptable to enemies and friends alike, and (3) it would need to encourage the development of the world community.

These goals which seemed impossible in 1967 today seem normal, rational, and even possible. Today (1990) one could consider that many of the following goals suggested by the AFSC Peace Education group have already been put into practice, or are being considered. We have helped, or are helping, Communist countries reach the amount of economic growth and development necessary for them to allow a degree of relaxed domestic control. We are helping Communist countries to achieve greater benefits through peaceful co-existence than they could receive through war. The goal of helping developing countries achieve social and political change has not as yet been achieved. Nor are we encouraging other nations to join in the development of one world.

The members of the Committee in *In Place of War* suggest that the world today is shaped by the needs of the weapons industries and, that the role of industry must be reversed so that its needs would depend on a "new" nonviolent foreign policy. A part of that program has already been suggested. Indeed, we hear laments from the military establishment as they anticipate cutbacks in their bases overseas as well as at home.

We have not as yet instituted the use of civilian defense teams. That might well become the work of the many peace groups throughout the western countries. But we have been using our peace institutions and our peace groups to instill such ideas as friendliness between nations. (Note the use of the term "friends" in the civilian peace group called "The American-Soviet Friendship Society.") We are attempting to help the emerging "new democratic" countries by contributing to their financial and economic systems.

American citizens, many of whom feared the USSR as an "evil empire" a few months ago, are now anticipating tourist visits to Moscow. Many of our school children are eagerly watching television documentaries concerning life within those countries previously considered as "enemy" nations.

Much is yet to be done by the peace groups and certainly by groups such as AFSC as well as the churches. It would be a mistake for any of those hard-working and dedicated citizen groups to think their work was finished. That work is, in fact, just now beginning.

The Report of Commission III at the Friends World Conference in 1937 on "Methods of Achieving Economic, Racial and International Justice" is as applicable today as it was then:

> The plight of native races and disadvantaged groups in Africa, India, Asia, Europe and America which so heavily weighed upon the minds and hearts of members of the Commission on Racial Justice, places both a responsibility and opportunity before the Society of Friends. Misunderstandings and bitterness which divide economic groups and national governments rest in no small measure upon race prejudice. If the causes of industrial and international wars are to be removed, effective work must be done in improving the status of disadvantaged groups.

Although frequently differing in method and attitude, members of the Society of Friends can do much in interpreting racial groups to each other and in removing the causes of misunderstanding. To do so they must be filled with a divine concern. They must lay that of God within themselves alongside the divine in [others] to build a richer and fuller life, regardless of race, or creed. In humility and forbearing love they must cast out fear, remove hypocrisy and banish hate from among themselves and those with whom they work. They must be diligent to assemble facts, unite in group endeavor and persist in effort to maintain justice, democracy and love in a world of increasing challenge and concern. (*Faith and Practice,* 1955).

REFERENCES

The Philadelphia Yearly Meeting of the Religious Society of Friends. *Faith and Practice*. Philadelphia: 1955.

Peace Education Division, AFSC. *In Place of War--An Inquiry Into Nonviolent Defense*. New York: Grossman, 1967.

Richard B. Gregg, *The Power of Nonviolence*. New York: Schocken, 1966.

Suggested Reading
(compiled by the editors)

Ahmad, Hazrat Mirza Tahir. *Murder in the Name of Allah.*
Cambridge, England: Lutterworth, 1990.

Altman, Nathaniel. *Ahimsa: Dynamic Compassion.* Wheaton:
Theosophical Publishing House, 1980.

Bing, Anthony K. *Israeli Pacifist: The Life of Joseph Abileah.*
Syracuse: University of Syracuse Press, 1990.

Brock, Peter. *Pacifism in the United States: From the Colonial
Era to the First World War.* Princeton: Princeton University
Press, 1968.

Chaplin, George and Glenn D. Paige, eds. *Hawaii 2000.*
Honolulu: University of Hawaii Press, 1973.

Cooney, Robert and Helen Michalowski. *Power of the People:
Active Nonviolence in the United States.* Philadelphia: New
Society, 1987. [Note: Chief Seattle's Message, pp. 6-7, has
recently been shown to be a screenwriter's fiction (1991)].

The Dalai Lama of Tibet. *Ocean of Wisdom.* San Francisco:
Harper & Row, 1990.

Easwaran, Eknath. *A Man to Match His Mountains: Badshah
Khan, Nonviolent Soldier of Islam.* Petaluma: Nilgiri, 1985.

Gandhi, M.K., ed. Abdul Majid Khan. *Fellowship of Faiths and
Unity of Religions.* New Delhi: Gandhi Book House, 1990.

Ikeda, Daisaku. *Life: An Enigma, a Precious Jewel.* Tokyo:
Kodansha International, 1982.

Ingram, Catherine. *In the Footsteps of Gandhi: Conversations with Spiritual Social Activists*. Berkeley: Parallax Press, 1990.

Jayatilleke, K.N. *Buddhism and Peace*. Kandy: Buddhist Publication Society, 1983.

King, Jr., Martin Luther. *Strength to Love*. New York: Harper & Row, 1963.

Knudsen-Hoffman, Gene, ed. *Ways Out: The Book of Changes for Peace*. Santa Barbara: John Daniel, 1988.

Kool, V.K. ed. *Perspectives on Nonviolence*. New York: Springer-Verlag, 1990.

Mayer, Peter, ed. *The Pacifist Conscience: Classic Writings on Alternatives to Violent Conflict From Ancient Times to the Present*. New York: Holt, Rinehart and Winston, 1966.

Merton, Thomas, ed. *Gandhi on Nonviolence*. New York: New Directions, 1965.

McSorley, Richard J. *New Testament Basis of Peacemaking*. Scottsdale, Pennsylvania: Herald Press, 1985.

Morgan, Kenneth. *Reaching for the Moon: On Asian Religious Paths*. Chambersburg, Pennsylvania: Anima Publications, 1990.

Perez Esquivel, Adolfo. *Christ in a Poncho*. Maryknoll: Orbis Books, 1983.

Roberts, Elizabeth and Elias Amidon, eds. *Earth Prayers*. New York: HarperCollins, 1991.

Saiyidain, K. G. *Islam: The Religion of Peace*. New Delhi: Islam & the Modern Age Society, 1976.

Scholl, Steven, ed. *The Peace Bible: Words from the Great Traditions.* Los Angeles: Kalimát Press, 1986.

Sharp, Gene. *The Politics of Nonviolent Action.* Boston: Porter Sargent, 1973.

Smith, Huston. *The Religions of Man.* New York: Harper & Row, 1989.

Solomonow, Allan, ed. *Roots of Jewish Nonviolence.* Nyack, New York: Jewish Peace Fellowship, 1988.

Thompson, Henry O. *World Religions in War and Peace.* Jefferson, North Carolina and London: McFarland, 1988.

Tolstoy, Leo. *The Kingdom of God is Within You.* London: Oxford University Press, 1974.

Tulsi, Acharya. *Bhagawan Mahavira: A Short Biography and Ideology of Lord Mahavira (599-527 B.C.), the Great Prophet of Jainism.* Ladnun, Rajasthan: Jain Vishva Bharati, 1985.

Tutu, Desmond. *Hope and Suffering.* Grand Rapids: William B. Eardmans, 1985.

Twain, Mark. *The War Prayer.* New York: Harper & Row, 1970.

Weinberg, Arthur and Lila, eds. *Instead of Violence: Writings of the Great Advocates of Peace and Nonviolence Throughout History.* Boston: Beacon, 1963.

Zahn, Gordon. *In Solitary Witness: The Life and Death of Franz Jägerstätter.* New York: Holt, Rinehart and Winston, 1964.

Contributors

Robert Aitken Rōshi studied with Nagakawa Soen Rōshi and Yasutani Hakuun Rōshi. In 1959 he and his wife Anne established a Zen organization, the Diamond Sangha, in Honolulu. Aitken was given the title "Rōshi" and authorized to teach by his teacher Yamada Koun Rōshi in 1974.

Reverend Stanley Amos is the Pastor at the Trinity Missionary Baptist Church in Honolulu. He received his Masters of Divinity from the Andover Newton Theological School. He is Executive Director of the Hawaii Afro-American Political Committee.

Ruth Anna Brown received a Ph.D. in Peace Education from The Susan B. Anthony University in 1987. She has been the Quaker Representative to the Coordinating Council for World Peace in Hawaii, as well as Clerk and Alternate Clerk of the Meeting.

Lou Ann Ha'aheo Guanson is an adventurer in nonviolence working to create a nonviolent community. She is co-founder of The Lighthouse, a fellowship of active nonviolence. Her academic background is in Social Ecology. Her research has focused particularly on creativity and leadership.

Ira Lichton is Professor of Human Nutrition in the University of Hawaii at Manoa. In 1962 he joined the Jewish Synagogue, Temple Emanu-El. He has served as President of the Synagogue (1973-1975), and as a trustee of the Jewish Federation of Hawaii.

Sister Anna McAnany belongs to the community of Maryknoll sisters. She has an M.A. degree in Theology from the University of Notre Dame. With the goal of global peace foremost in her mind, she works in peace education among students on the Waianae coast. She also trains teachers and religious educators in peace education skills.

Tony Pelle is a member of the nine member governing body of the Hawaii Baha'i Spiritual Assembly, as well as its Public Information Director. He served as Public Information Director for the U.S. Army and Air Force around the world and in the U.S. Space Program. He retired with the rank of Colonel after 25 years of service.

Wasim Siddiqui is a Boardmember of the Muslim Association of Hawaii. He is Professor and Chair of the Tropical Medicine and Medical Microbiology Department in the University of Hawaii at Manoa.

H.H. Sivaya Subramuniyaswami is the Founder and President of both the Saiva Siddhanta Church and the Himalayan Academy. He is also the Publisher of "Hinduism Today"--an international Hindu newspaper published in the United States, Malaysia, Mauritius, South Africa, Fiji Islands, and Holland.

Editors

Glenn D. Paige serves as coordinator of the Center for Global Nonviolence Planning Project, Spark M. Matsunaga Institute for Peace, University of Hawaii and is Professor of Political Science in the University of Hawaii at Manoa. He is co-editor with George Chaplin of *Hawaii 2000* (1973), and is editor of *Buddhism and Leadership for Peace* (1984). He convened a United Nations University exploratory seminar on "Islam and Nonviolence" in Bali (1986) and gave the Third Annual Gandhi Memorial Lecture in New Delhi on October 26, 1990. He serves also on the national advisory board of the New York State Martin Luther King Jr. Institute of Nonviolence.

Sarah Gilliatt is a student of Buddhism. She focuses on the relationship between Buddhism and peace. She is co-editor with Snjezana Akpinar of *A Buddhist Philosophy of Religion* (1991).

Index

Abdu'l-Baha, 15, 17-8, 19. *See also* Baha'i.

Abel, *See* Cain and.

actions, 3, 10, 26, 27-8, 33, 34-5, 50, 51, 59, 60, 68, 69, 71.

Agape, 46. *See also* love.

ahimsa, def. of, 50-1. *See also* Hinduism; nonviolence.

aina, 6, 9, 10. *See also* earth; environment; Hawaiian spiritual tradition.

alo, 5.

aloha, 5-6, 8. *See also* Hawaiian spiritual tradition; love.

Amos, 77.

anger, 6, 9, 10, 19, 20-1, 55, 58, 60, 61, 62, 63, 85, 89.

Anthony, Susan B., 82.

arms race, 46.

atom bomb, 44, 90. *See also* arms race; disarmament; war.

Augustine, St., 44.

Avalokiteshvara, *See* compassion.

Bab, 13. *See also* Baha'i.

Baha'ullah, 13, 14, 15, 18, 21. *See also* Baha'i.

Baha'i: causes of nonviolence, 16-7, 15-6, 16-7; causes of violence, 13-4, 15-6, 16-7; characteristics of nonviolent society, 21-3; community in, 17;   education theory, 14, 19; "encouragement," 17, 20; environment, attitude toward, 14, 15, 18; faith, 20; history of, 13; in Iran, 13, 14; justice in, 14, 19, 21; love in, 14, 17, 18, 19, 20, 21; and nonviolence, 14-15, 16-8, 19, 20-1; principles of,

13-4; transition to nonviolent society, 18, 20-1; and violence, 13, 14, 15, 17-8, 19.

Base Communities, 31.

Berlin Wall, 89.

Berrigan, Daniel and Philip, 47.

Borge, Tomas, 47.

Brook Farm, 31.

Buddha, 87; *See also* Buddhism.

Buddhism: *bodhisattva,* 28, 29; community *(sangha)* in, 30-1; compassion in, 26, 27-30; cooperative movements, 31; Eightfold Path, 25-7, 30; Four Noble Truths, 25; *Hua-yen Sutra,* 27-8; interdependence, theory of, 25, 26, 27-8, 29; Kuan-yin (Kannon), 29-30; Maitreya, 27, 29, 30; personalization of teachings, 28-30; Pu-tai (Hotei), 29-30; vow of non-harm, 30-1.

Cain and Abel, 35.

capital punishment, 46, 47.

Catholic Worker, 31.

Christ, Jesus, 35, 40, 41, 42, 45, 46, 83, 84, 88; first coming of, 36.

Christianity: St. Augustine, 44; community in, 35, 37, 39, 43, 44; Day, Dorothy, 45, 47; environment, attitude toward, 47; Gandhi, 43; God, 36, 37, 38, 39, 47; Jesus, 35, 40, 41, 42, 45, 46; and justice, 40, 41, 42, 48; King, Jr. Martin Luther, 37, 48; love in, 35, 37, 38, 40, 41, 43, 44, 45, 48; and nonviolence, 33-4, 37, 39-40; Sermon on the Mount, 35, 40, 43; and violence,